Teens SHARE the Mission

Compiled and edited by
the Daughters of St. Paul

Foreword by Britt Leigh

Pauline
BOOKS & MEDIA
Boston

Library of Congress Cataloging-in-Publication Data

Teens share the mission / compiled and edited by the Daughters of St. Paul ; foreword by Britt Leigh.

    pages cm

  ISBN 978-0-8198-7509-9 -- ISBN 0-8198-7509-0 1. Youth in missionary work. I. Daughters of St. Paul.

  BV2617.T44 2014

  266.00835--dc23

2014003904

The Scripture quotations contained herein are from the *New Revised Standard Version Bible: Catholic Edition,* copyright © 1989, 1993, Division of Christian Education of the National Council of the Churches of Christ in the United States of America. Used by permission. All rights reserved.

Excerpts from the English translation of the *Catechism of the Catholic Church* for use in the United States of America, copyright © 1994, United States Catholic Conference, Inc. —Libreria Editrice Vaticana. Used with permission.

Cover design by Mary Joseph Peterson, FSP

Cover photo istockphoto.com/franckreporter

Published by Pauline Books & Media, 50 Saint Pauls Avenue, Boston, MA 02130–3491

Printed in the U.S.A.

www.pauline.org

Pauline Books & Media is the publishing house of the Daughters of St. Paul, an international congregation of women religious serving the Church with the communications media.

1 2 3 4 5 6 7 8 9   18 17 16 15 14

"Evangelizing

is the

Church's mission.

It is **not**

the mission of **only a few**,

but it is *MINE*,

YOURS,

and *OUR* mission.**"**

Pope Francis,
General Audience,
May 22, 2013

FOREWORD

When I was a teen not so long ago, I did lots of service hours. I'm talking tons. I don't know how many service hours I had by the end of high school, but it must have been somewhere in the hundreds or thousands. I mean, I got *awards* for them! Now, mind you, I did not volunteer with the mission of "I want to get an award" but "I enjoy doing this, it takes care of a requirement, and hey, people are helped—so everyone feels good!" But it took *waaay* longer than it should have to realize what my true mission was and how my true reward was so much more than any paper certificates could be.

Mission is a call from God to serve his people. It's a call to serve *his* mission to go out into the world, spread the Gospel, and make new disciples. Mission is more than just a service project, volunteer hours, or trip to a foreign country. Mission can be praying with a friend who's upset, writing about your faith on a blog, or doing extra chores for your dad. Mission is mission when, in the spirit of Christ Jesus, you share God's love to the world. Mission is about those you serve, *not about you*.

Of course being on mission can be something you already enjoy doing and can make you feel all warm and fuzzy inside. But God is calling you and your work to a higher purpose: he wants you to feel the joy of helping others just for the sake of the others, to continue helping others feel good—even when you're not. Because our "reward" for mission isn't meeting some hours requirement or recognition—it's that God was made present to someone who needs him.

In this book, you'll hear from teens like you who have started on their missions, serving others in many different ways. After each story, there are two prompts for reflection. Take some time to think on them, pray with them, and act on them. Some will just be questions to consider about yourself, your relationship with God, and your own mission. Others might have Scripture quotes or other churchy things to look up, so it might be helpful to have a Bible handy. If you're not near the Internet to look stuff up, don't worry; you can always come back to them later. There's no set order to read them in or work through them. Pick a new story or question. For those writerly types like yours truly, you can journal your answers.

Now that I'm all "grown up," I continue to serve. And God continues to work on my mind and heart. The way God asks me to be of service to others has shifted in terms of what I do and how I do it. Now I serve with the ever-present focus of "How is this mission? How is this benefiting God's people and bringing them closer to him?" The call to mission is ongoing; there is no final stop; the work is never over. But right here, right now, in this time of your lives, God is calling you. Get ready to listen, prepare yourself, and respond to him.

Pope Francis believes you are the best person for the job. In his closing homily at World Youth Day 2013, he said, "Do you know what the best tool is for evangelizing the young? Another young person. This is the path to follow! . . . The Church needs you, your enthusiasm, your creativity and the joy that is so characteristic of you."

Well, what do you say? Are you ready to share the mission?

Go.

—*Britt Leigh, author of the teen novel*
Ten Commandments for Kissing Gloria Jean

JOY

A Bolivian sun will burn Caucasians. I should know; I'm really quite fair-skinned, and I did get burned some, though a hat and 45 SPF sunscreen a few times a day kept the burn at a minimum. The sun is no trouble for Bolivians; their beautiful brown faces have borne it since the days of the Incas. Their dark eyes have a shape that looked mournful to me. They have wise old faces, worn by years of oppression and poverty in a country where 70 percent are poor. But once they smiled, the age disappeared and joy filled their features.

Seventeen of us stayed at a parish two hours away from Santa Cruz, a city in the eastern part of Bolivia. We visited communities with the padre when he made Mass rounds, fixed up a chapel, visited an orphanage, and helped with children's games. I remember so much: the friendships, the people, the poverty that had most of us in tears . . . But there was such faith, too; faith in God alive in the community. I am often asked which part of the experience was best, and I don't know what to say. It was all so wonderful, and sad, and joyous all at once that my response is only, "The people. So giving and welcoming. I cried when we left; most of us did."

I will always remember the joy of my new Bolivian friends, the *jovenes* (youths) of Buena Vista. Whether they were teaching us a Bolivian cheering chant, or learning "Boom Chicka Boom" from us (I think we started a new trend), they were very happy. Those beautiful brown people with sad-shaped eyes taught me joy. Joy is elusive; sometimes it's not found even in the noblest of pursuits. But these people, all of whom were so willing, so happy, so self-giving, so Christ-like, understood joy and gave it freely.

Going to Bolivia, I knew I could never give more than receive—but I never expected to feel like I had done so little. Maybe that's how the apostles felt listening to Christ—like they'd done nothing but be filled with God's love, joy, and hope.

—Alice

For Reflection

✳ There's a great acronym for understanding joy: Jesus, Others, Yourself. How does what you do every day model Jesus? What are you doing for others? How are you joyful?

✳ We all like the feeling of accomplishment when we've finished something particularly hard. Sometimes, however, it seems like we've actually done very little. Challenge yourself to see the joy, hope, and love of God in all that you do—or don't do.

SERVICE OF PRESENCE

I had entered an entirely different world. The air was warm and humid, not chilly; and the locals spoke Spanish, not English. The poverty I witnessed was something I had never encountered before. It was as if I had fallen out of *my* world—a world focused on me—and had dropped into God's world.

With other high school seniors and some teachers, I volunteered in the San Salvador area of El Salvador for a week. There I helped mix cement for a new house and classroom, paint a daycare, and laughed and played with local children. But mostly, I learned about the importance of human love.

I loved these Salvadorans, even though I had known them for only a week. It seemed as though I had known them my entire life. They helped me to know myself better and to see God's role in my life. It didn't matter if I was playing board games with the kids, joking with the adults, or pouring cement, I just felt so blessed to be there. Those we interacted with gave us love, comfort, and encouragement. I wanted to do so much more for them than was possible in one week.

Despite all the "things" we did, our team discovered that the most important service we provided was the "service of presence." We learned that we provided comfort for those in pain and those living in poverty by simply being there and showing them that they are neither forgotten nor alone. They thanked us repeatedly for our help, while I felt as though I should be expressing my gratitude to them.

What the Salvadorans needed most was our community. I found I needed it, too. One afternoon, after a long day of cement mixing, a local man helped me clean my shovel. Let me explain: cleaning a shovel is an activity for one person. You just pour some water over the blade and scrape at the cement residue with a rock. Some might have considered the man's help to be no big deal, but it was important to me. Maybe it's because of our North American individualistic culture, or maybe it's because I can be a little "closed-off" at times, but this man taking the time to help me touched my life. I didn't *need* his help but he gave it anyway.

I remember frequently the friends I made in El Salvador. I often wish I could return there, but, as Mother Teresa once observed, love begins by taking care of the closest ones—the ones at home. So now I am beginning to rediscover love here at home. The "service of presence" that I gave in El Salvador I can also give to those here at home however I am able. I can love strangers, my friends, and my family, right here at home. I can support them in many ways, even with something as insignificant as cleaning off a shovel.

—Rachel

For Reflection

❋ In what ways are you "closed off" and how can you share yourself and your gifts with others?

❋ Who do you know that could benefit from the "service of presence?"

LIVING THE FAITH

I think back on three days that impacted my life forever. I had been asked to help lead an eighth grade Confirmation retreat at my parish, Blessed Teresa of Calcutta. I was told I'd help with small and large group discussions, games, and service projects. When I was first asked to be one of the leaders on this retreat, I was scared. But I also felt compelled by the Spirit to help, and so I agreed.

The topics we'd covered were chastity, "masks," relationships with God, forgiveness, and alcohol and drugs. While telling others about the dangers of high school, I learned that I had gotten so caught up in them that instead of thanking God for every day of my life, I blamed him for every single one. That weekend, for the first time in four years, I went to confession and I completely broke down. The priest who was there gave me the best advice I have ever received. To this day I remember every word he spoke to me.

Over the course of the weekend I was asked several questions about my faith. And when I shared personal stories about my relationship with God, it really made me focus on where I stood with him. I was a senior in high school and I couldn't have felt more lost; I had no sense of direction when it came to my faith. Six months after that retreat I understood that *I* was meant to be there. That weekend was not about me teaching those kids, but about them teaching me.

That weekend God healed my faith and brought me closer to him than I could have ever imagined. Looking back there are some things I wish I could have done differently. It is up to us whether or not to accept God's invitation to serve others and allow God to touch us through that service. People have said to me, "Wow, you love God." And now, yes, I can proudly say, "I love God!" For that I owe him all my praises.

—Grace B.

For Reflection

✴ What is the Holy Spirit asking you to do that might seem overwhelming or frightening? Do you trust God to provide you with the skills and resources you need to follow his invitation of service?

✴ What unexpected lessons has the Holy Spirit taught you?

THE HOUSE
OF SACRIFICE

Each semester my youth group hosts an overnight service lock-in during which we teens do corporal works of mercy for our community on a regular basis. These lock-ins consist of an evening reflecting on the gifts God has given us and, on the following day, a full day of working with a local charity. Usually these events are a lot of fun because you have your friends around. One semester, we were going to help a charity that builds homes for people who can't afford them. I was very familiar with the organization, so I wasn't expecting anything new or any surprises. Boy, was I wrong!

On a very hot and sunny day we arrived at a house that seemed fine on the outside. But the inside and back yard was another matter. Broken cabinets were hanging by a single nail, buckled tiles on the floor begged to be replaced, and there was a mountain of rocks in the backyard.

There were around thirty-five teens, two chaperones, a man who was in charge of the construction, and a lady. It was nonstop hard labor for many hours for all of us, a level of labor which I was not accustomed to doing. We had to demolish cabinets, rip out tile, and move a tremendous amount of rock under the scorching sun. I started to regret volunteering. I just wanted to be sitting in my air-conditioned home instead.

After finishing the work we were asked to do, we gathered in the front yard. The man in charge thanked us for our help and then asked the lady to speak. We found out then that she was the prospective owner of the house. She was so appreciative of our help with her future home, that she started crying. It was at that point that I realized what sacrifice can do. The numerous hours that we sacrificed in the hot sun were for a person. I realized that since Jesus Christ sacrificed his life for us, then I can sacrifice something to help my brothers and sisters. My experience taught me the importance of service, and augmented my faith by widening my appreciation of Christ's sacrifice for us.

—Jim

For Reflection

✳ Take a moment to reflect on the sacrifice Jesus made for us, for you. What sacrifice, such as the strenuous manual labor in the story, are you reluctant to undertake?

✳ Jim was able to hear from the prospective home owner words of gratitude, but that isn't the reason why he volunteered. What can you do today as a corporal act of mercy without waiting for the reward of gratitude?

SPEAK OPENLY

I have always liked helping others, whether it's donating clothes that no longer fit, packaging food and shipping it to poor countries, giving to charity, or just lending a helping hand. Work Camp, however, would be a new level of volunteering—one that would allow me to see the direct result I had on someone's life.

As the date drew near, my worries about Work Camp escalated. A week of working in the hot sun with people I have never met and sleeping on the floor on my twin-sized air mattress was more than I thought I could handle. I remember thinking that I needed to have faith in God that this would be a week worth remembering.

On the first day of Work Camp I met the four teens I would be spending the next week of my life with. It was a great relief to find out that they had the same concerns I had about work camp. We had been told that the journey would not be easy, but the reward would be great. Still, as my crew and I arrived at the run-down trailer home with a swarm of wasps, we were a little taken aback.

As the week progressed, however, my faith grew stronger and the trailer's condition greatly improved. I was amazed by the transformation of not only the trailer, but of myself. Most days when we took our lunch break we would pray and talk about the feelings and experiences we had. We would also talk about why we thought God put us in that situation. I was surprised by how comfortable everyone was talking about God and their faith. Being one of the very few Catholic girls at my school, people speaking openly about their Catholic faith wasn't something I heard very often. It felt good to be able to speak openly and to see the change our work could enable.

For me, this experience allowed me to see a side of God that I hadn't seen before. I feel that God blessed me through this experience by showing me that there are other people in the world that share my faith and want to be an instrument of God's goodness and love.

—*Danielle*

For Reflection

✳ What difficult journeys—physical or spiritual—have you taken? What were the results?

✳ What are some reasons people are afraid to speak openly about their faith, about God? What can be done to overcome this fear?

SPECIAL FRIENDS

Sitting in my junior year religion class I listened to a presentation about a home for abused children located in St. Louis, Missouri. We were told about "Special Friends," a project to get kids there to open up and help them realize that there are people who care. Those who signed up would go every Wednesday for a year and hang out with their assigned friend(s) for two hours. I love kids—they're so energetic and fun to be around—so I signed up.

The first time I went to the program I was surprised. I was unprepared for the roomful of shy, quiet, and uncertain faces. I was assigned to be a friend to three boys. The first few weeks I went, the kids in the program were very quiet and many were angry, particularly with God.

By the second month they began to open up and realize that what had happened to them wasn't God's fault. Slowly the shyness and quietness began to melt away. They began sharing secrets, telling me stories, calling out my name when I walked in, hugging me goodbye, and even telling me they loved me and were thankful I came.

As the end of the year drew closer, my three special friends could tell that I was sad. When they asked me why, I told them that it was because my time with them was almost over. They responded that regardless of how much time would pass, we would always be friends because Jesus willed it. I didn't want to leave. Being with them was nothing but pure happiness. Each time I walked into that room to be with the kids, I felt like I had walked into the presence of God.

This experience taught me that service isn't just about helping those around you, but also helping yourself. Former UCLA basketball coach John Wooden once said, "You can't live a perfect day without doing something for someone who will never be able to repay you." I totally agree; I have come to understand that in service you find yourself, your faith, and God himself.

—Grace B.

For Reflection

✳ Who are your friends? What brought you together? What keeps your friendship alive? Think about the people Jesus may be calling you to befriend, even if they are different from you. How can new friendships with these people enrich the friendships you already have?

✳ We will encounter many people distant from God, especially when we serve. How might you respond when someone expresses their anger or disappointment toward God or the Church?

MISSION AT HOME

"Can you get me a glass of water?"

"Would you please change the baby's diaper?"

"Take out the garbage, please."

"Help your brother with his schoolwork."

"Please clean your room."

I spend a lot of time at home, and I have found that God's mission for me often entails using the "boring" moments of regular life creatively for him. I hate doing disgusting chores and repetitive tasks (I'm positive I'll never like doing them); but, it is possible for me to use them for something more. Oftentimes I feel that the Holy Spirit prompts me to offer up my frustrations and impatience so that God can use them to further his mission. Usually this lessens my bad mood and makes what I'm doing more enjoyable.

Offering the whole day as a prayer, regardless of where or how you live, is the best sort of mission. This practice has taught me to see the little tasks and general busyness of ordinary life as God sees them: they are part of a much larger masterpiece. My home is a great place to serve Christ. Everyday menial tasks, when offered to Jesus, can become an extraordinary sacrifice for the salvation of many. Instead of griping always about washing the dishes or doing the laundry, doing them cheerfully and offering that to God for a sick neighbor or my parish priest gives purpose to the sacrifice.

This mission may seem simple but it requires trust. I can only do it by relying on God for strength and courage, and the saints for inspiration. My home mission is not exciting or easy, but it can be rewarding.

—*Marie V.*

For Reflection

✻ Blessed Mother Teresa of Calcutta is attributed with writing, "Stay where you are. Find your own Calcutta. Find the sick, the suffering, and the lonely right there where you are—in your own homes and in your own families, in your workplaces and in your schools." What are some needs in your community? How can you serve the people in your neighborhood and school?

✻ "It is no use walking anywhere to preach unless our walking is our preaching," said Saint Francis of Assisi. How is the Lord inviting you to make your daily life and its chores—your walking—a witness to Christ?

SEEING GOD'S WORK
IN PROGRESS

For the past three years, I have been blessed to be on LIFE Team, the campus ministry program, at my high school. Being a leader for the freshman class retreat allowed me to see things beyond my own experiences and opened up my eyes to people from many walks of life. The retreat, entitled "A Teen's Game Plan for Life," was a two-day retreat during which the participants and those leading them had the opportunity to grow closer to one another and God.

I loved working this retreat because I got to see God's work in progress. One of my favorite moments during the retreat was when we had adoration of the Blessed Sacrament under the stars. Many of the freshmen had never experienced adoration, and it was beautiful to see their faces filled with awe and wonder as they prayed. For me, seeing them gather in front of the Lord as a family and understanding that we are one in communion with the Lord was breathtaking. By the end of the night many of the freshmen had experienced Jesus in their hearts. We could feel his light shining through one another.

At times, I wonder why the Lord has placed and kept me on this path. Being part of leading this retreat has helped me to be more compassionate, have a better prayer life, and remain grounded in the Lord. It has given me the knowledge and understanding of how to be more like Christ. Wherever I go from here, my experiences will remind me that "I am who I am because of who he is."

—AnaLexicis

For Reflection

✳ Have you ever made a retreat or spent time in Eucharistic adoration or prayer when it wasn't required? If so, what inspired you to go? If you have not, what do you think prevents you from setting aside the time?

✳ In who, what, where, when, or how do you see God at work in others? How can you challenge yourself to see God's work in progress in *you*?

WHAT LOVE LOOKS LIKE

I woke up feeling tired, sore, and by no means ready to face another eight hours of hard work in El Chonco, a community just north of Chinandega, Nicaragua. As I shut my eyes and silently begged for just five more minutes of sleep, I remembered that it was my day on PB&J duty. Making sandwiches for the 100 other missionaries working with "Amigos for Christ" was a task I dreaded.

This was my second year helping in El Chonco. As I sat down in the school's brand new feeding center, I felt a light tap on my shoulder. I turned to see William—a boy I had befriended the previous summer—standing with his sister, Lacey. In a quiet voice, he asked me, *"¿Puedo ayudarte?"* ("Can I help you?").

I happily handed the two of them a loaf of bread and two jars of peanut butter and jelly, thinking, *"Hey, if they make the sandwiches, I won't have to."*

After giving the kids a quick PB&J-making crash course, I watched as Lacey took a squeeze bottle of jelly and William a slice of bread. Lacey then squeezed the jelly tube above the bread in William's hands and SPLAT—jelly went everywhere, oozing all over William's hands. Before I could start cleaning the mess, Lacey threw her head back and laughed. Before I knew it William was laughing uncontrollably, too. Then, before long I joined in; the three of us couldn't stop.

When I finally got my laughter under control, I watched William and Lacey continue to laugh and sat in awe of this beautiful, profound moment of pure joy. It was the kind of joy that only God can create; moments of pure magic where we feel God's presence most. To me, the joy I witnessed is what love looks like.

In the simple witnessing of shared laughter I felt that I experienced God most profoundly. I learned that any given situation can be an opportunity to experience God's love, no matter how miserable the task may seem. The smiling, laughing faces of William and Lacey are forever imprinted on my heart; they are constant reminders to me that God is joy, and joy can be found in the simplest moments. All we have to do is open our eyes and allow our hearts to come alive, just as mine did that day in Nicaragua.

—Emily

For Reflection

✸ In Saint Paul's second letter to the Corinthians it says, "Each of you must give as you have made up your mind, not reluctantly or under compulsion, for God loves a cheerful giver" (2 Cor 9:7). What is the Lord asking you, in this moment, to commit to totally and cheerfully?

✸ When was the last time you experienced the joy of God? Ask him for more simple moments and people to "bring your heart alive."

COURAGE FROM GOD

After experiencing my own freshman retreat, I knew that I also wanted to help with campus ministry. I helped out in various ways for a few years, and then I was asked to give a testimony talk for the freshmen during their retreat. My initial response to the request was to say "no." I didn't think this was something I could do. Our campus minister, however, would not take "no" for an answer. Eventually I agreed.

Preparing for my talk, I knew I could only get the courage I needed from God. I trusted God to help me decide what to say as well as the courage and wisdom to share those words with others. After a lot of prayer and meditation, I felt ready to give the testimony.

When the time came for me to speak, I was so nervous I could feel my heart beating like crazy. But once I began to speak, the nerves began to go away.

The best part of the experience for me was hearing all of the positive feedback I received from the freshman class. Knowing that my words changed a few minds was the best feeling I could have ever felt. I believe that God guided me and helped write the testimony he was asking me to give.

—Talegria

For Reflection

✳ Sharing personal stories can be intimidating, especially when it comes to saying something about a personal relationship with God. If you were asked to give a testimony or witness talk, what would you choose to talk about?

✳ Why is it important to allow God to help guide us in the choices we make when speaking? Ask God today to help you be a witness of all he has done for you.

THE GIFT OF COLORS

Every year my hometown parish, Blessed Teresa of Calcutta, takes a group of kids on a mission trip. When I found out the group would be helping the Appalachian people of West Virginia, I knew right away I wanted to go. I wanted to make a difference in people's lives and share the gifts God has given me. Little did I know the difference they would make in my life.

I remember the day we pulled into the area we would be working on all week. It looked dilapidated: trash piled up, overgrown weeds, broken windows, and much more. It was nothing like I was used to in my neighborhood. At one house we met a man (who went by the name of Coach), and his wife. Coach's wife asked us to paint the outside of their house fuchsia. It seemed like an odd color choice, but we did it without question.

Later that day, we noticed that the couple's basement was baby blue; the living room, lime green; and the bathroom, sunshine yellow. Seeing we were shocked by all the "outrageous" colors, Coach's wife told us God gave her the gift of colors and she loved them all. Her words opened my eyes. Despite the incredible poverty that she lived in, this woman still looked at the bright side of things and praised God for what she had. Then I noticed that whenever her neighbors walked by her house they would smile. Coach's wife brought light and smiles to her town with her love of God's colors. Coach's wife's faith was so strong she helped us volunteers and her neighbors believe God's love was present.

I signed up for that week of service because I thought I would be helping people, but they ended up helping me. Coach's wife and other townspeople taught me that God is always present in our lives if we choose to make him seen. So, regardless of whether I was painting, chopping down trees, building steps, or tearing off siding, God was there.

This experience made me want to continue doing service. I hope that just like Coach's wife did for me, others will also come to know Christ through whatever I do. In a sense, you could say I want to "pay the faith forward."

—*Grace B.*

For Reflection

✳ Think about a person whose faith has brightened your day. What can you do to make your own faith more vibrant when you "pay it forward?"

✳ Since God created the world, we are able to "see" God in all things. Some people experience God in art, or in nature, or in people watching. Today, take a walk and look at the world and its people around you. Pray for all you see.

UNIVERSAL

Two summers ago, I had the opportunity to go on a week-long service trip to Belize in Central America with seven other girls. I have always loved doing service work and was extremely excited to have the chance to help in another country. We were sent to help a small village plaster the outside walls of their newly constructed church. We had to cover the bricks with a cement mixture we made ourselves so that the people of the village could then paint it.

The work was extremely physically taxing, but I wouldn't have traded a single minute of the experience. From trying to figure out how to go to the bathroom in the middle of the jungle, to playing with the village children during our lunch break, every moment of our week was a moment I treasure.

As much fun as this trip was, the best part was being able to see the faith of the people of this rural community. One day, we went to Mass in a very isolated village, near the village in which we were working. It was amazing to see how many people walked for hours just to be able to attend a weekday Mass.

Because of my experiences in Belize I was able to understand what it means when we say that the word "catholic" means "universal." Even though our life-styles are so different from theirs, I was able to feel a connection with the people there through the beliefs we share. This trip was an experience that strength-ened my passion and desire to serve, and I hope to someday return to Belize.

—Lydia

For Reflection

✳ What is your experience of Mass and Church where you live? How does it affect your faith? Visit another parish and see what's the same and what's different. Think about how the experience of going to Mass might be different in other parts of the world.

✳ The word "catholic" means universal. The Church is meant to be universal. Think of an experience you have had of that universality. How is God inviting you today to serve our *universal* Church?

EXPERIENCING CHRIST THROUGH MUSIC

One day, after my lesson, my piano teacher asked me if I wanted to help her and her friend with a sing-along at the local nursing home. They did this every Tuesday. At the time I was in fourth grade and was a little nervous. I asked my mom if I could go even though the sing-along was in the middle of the day. Since I was being homeschooled, my mom thought it would be a good idea for me to help.

That simple invitation kick-started an addictive ministry. For the next two years I sang and played piano at the nursing home every single Tuesday. When I turned eleven, my teacher asked me to play for Sunday Mass once a month there. Now, I happily continue that service and love it more than anything else I do musically.

My piano teacher's simple invitation is one of the best things that has ever happened to me. Why?

Because when I began to help I was worried and afraid about interacting with the elderly. But it taught me about the dignity of each person. God tells us not to be afraid numerous times in the Bible; and he meant it. As I got to know the residents and listened to their stories my fear melted rapidly.

This ministry gave me so much more than a simple opportunity to practice my music skills. I learned to see Christ in all people, even those that I thought couldn't understand me. I soon found that these people understood me better than some others because they had wisdom and experience due to their age. I've grown close to many of them. The nursing home residents have dignity and deserve my absolute best. From the start I could tell that they loved me. I just loved them back.

I have been serving at the nursing home in multiple ways for six years now. God has blessed me in more ways than I could possibly imagine. I love being there, working with the residents and experiencing Christ through the music I play and his people gathered to enjoy it. I have learned that if

God calls a person to do something, nothing—not even fear—can overcome God's grace. Love always conquers fear, and then joy abounds.

—*Marie V.*

For Reflection

✳ Our talents are gifts from God. As such, we must accept these gifts in order to use them. What talent is God inviting you to put at the service of the Church? How can you bring your skills to the next level, and what would you do with what you've learned?

✳ Recognizing the dignity each person has is one of the greatest things we can do for one another. How is God asking you to look beyond your preconceived notions in your actions toward and with others?

AS SIMPLE AS A CONVERSATION

I believe that, in God's mysterious and wonderful plan, he puts us in specific places for specific reasons. This revelation became as clear as day for me when I volunteered during the second semester of my freshman year of college at a hospital in Richmond, Virginia. We were allowed to choose an area of the hospital to work in, so I picked Palliative Care. It's a unit dedicated to the pain management of those who are recovering from a serious illness or dying.

I committed to a two-hour shift once a week. The more time I spent there, the more I learned how peaceful and welcoming the people and staff of Palliative Care were. The unit's directors made it feel like a home away from home by maintaining an in-unit kitchen—decorated with butterflies to symbolize hope—and creating a warm environment through actions and attitude. I also enjoyed enlightening morning talks and time together with two gregarious senior volunteers who became my friends.

But there is one memory that sticks out the most. One cloudy morning, a middle aged woman walked into the kitchen area where I was preparing coffee and tea. She looked quite solemn and resigned, as if her troubles were too much to bear. I could tell that she had been crying from her slightly swollen eyes. As with anyone who walked into the kitchen, I offered her something to drink. I watched as the senior volunteer started up a simple conversation with her about where she lived. After a little bit, I joined in, too. In a matter of minutes the lady was leading the conversation, telling us about her life history, her family, and even the touchy subject of why she was in the hospital. She confided that her husband had been in Palliative Care for a while, and it seemed that his recovery was unlikely.

As our conversation continued, her sorrowful disposition was replaced with budding vitality and hope. It was fascinating to see how much this conversation was helping this lady. With every word that was said, I felt like her troubles were streaming out of her, if only for that moment. I am glad that I was there for her that day as a volunteer, because it showed me how something as simple as a conversation can do so much.

—*Cyrelle*

For Reflection

❋ On suffering, the *Catechism of the Catholic Church* says, "Our experiences of faith and suffering, injustice and death, seem to contradict the Good News; they can shake our faith and become a temptation against it. It is then we must turn to the *witnesses of faith. . .*" (CCC 164, 165). Everyone experiences suffering on some level. Think of a time when you suffered. Did your faith help you live that time with hope? If not, how could it have?

❋ Just as the woman in this story did, Saint Paul shared with the people of Corinth some of his many trials:

But whatever anyone dares to boast of . . . I also dare to boast of that . . . with far greater labors, far more imprisonments, with countless floggings,

and often near death. Five times I have received
from the Jews the forty lashes minus one. Three
times I was beaten with rods. Once I received a
stoning. Three times I was shipwrecked; for a night
and a day I was adrift at sea; on frequent journeys,
in danger from rivers, danger from bandits, danger
from my own people . . . in toil and hardship,
through many a sleepless night, hungry and
thirsty, often without food, cold and naked. . . .
(2 Cor 11: 21, 23–27)

How has God intervened in your life? What experiences has God given you that touched you deeply?

WITH GOD
IN THE ANDES

"Truly I tell you, just as you did it to one of the least of these who are members of my family, you did it to me" (Mt 25:40). This is the guiding Scripture verse for the Project Matthew 25:40 missionaries. One summer I went with a group of nineteen people who embarked on a two-week mission to the High Andes in Cuzco, Peru, where we volunteered with an order called The Missionary Servants of the Poor of the Third World.

I wanted to go not only to serve the poor, but I also wanted to learn how to see the face of Christ in the poor. I didn't know what to expect, but God is so good and I trusted that he would make everything turn out fine.

The job the girls were assigned to usually involved children, which I found to be a huge blessing. Most of our days were spent with the children at a school. Our evenings were spent with children living in an orphanage. I was assigned the San Rafael

Room, the baby room, in the orphanage. There were about fifteen boys and girls ranging in age from newborn to a year old. Some of these children had disabilities and deformities such as hydrocephaly, cerebral palsy, cleft lip, and cleft palate.

There was a special boy at the orphanage whose name was Juan Gabriel. He was nine months old when we arrived, but he was about the size of a newborn. Something inside of him prevented his growth and caused him to have a hard time eating. Because of his condition, Juan Gabriel suffered greatly—a suffering that was evident in his tiny face. Regardless of the pain, he hardly ever cried. He just lay quietly in his crib and waited for someone to feed, clothe, or hold him.

After I returned home I realized that Juan Gabriel was the face of the suffering Christ I had gone in search of. A small, sick baby in an orphanage high up in the Andes, hidden away in a small room; he was the face of Christ. I realized that you don't have to look for God in large places. Sometimes an orphanage in a tiny mountain village is the perfect place to start looking for God. Not long after we returned home, I heard that Juan Gabriel had died. But every time I think of him, I realize how blessed I am to have been able to see, hold, and touch him every day I was there.

Besides doing many corporal works of mercy, saying lots of prayers, and doing a lot of work for the mission, I realized something. I wasn't the one serving, I was the one *being served*. When we would go to the mud huts to visit families, they offered us all they had for dinner—roasted beans. They gave to us because they saw us as Christ. When I turned to shake hands at the sign of peace, I received a big hug instead. I realized that despite the fact that I was richer in material things than the people I met in Peru, they were richer spiritually. I learned that the Church is alive and well, maybe even better, in the most remote places of the world.

Mission service taught me that it wasn't all about me. It was about God. I learned so much and gained so much, and yet it seems I gave so little. It seems all God really wants is a "yes" and an open heart, and he will show you his face in big and little ways.

—*Mary Clare*

For Reflection

✳ The Blessed Mother Mary said "yes" to God and trusted in his call for her. What does God want you to say yes to? Do you trust him? Talk with him about it.

✳ Think of someone who has been the face of Christ for you. How has this person's witness shaped and molded you? How did you respond to him or her? How does God want you to respond?

IT'S NOT ALL ABOUT ME

Life doesn't always revolve around us. That can be a hard lesson to learn. As children we grow up being the center of attention. The sound of a cry was like an alarm going off to our parents and they would run to the rescue. At least it was like that for me. As I grew into a young adult I had to learn it wasn't always about me. High school was like a big slap in the face. I joined a youth ministry program and was soon asked to help out with the middle school youth group.

I learned that the first rule of ministry is serving someone other than yourself—that ministry wasn't about me at all. I grew up thinking that I was the center of the world, but in helping with the middle school youth group I suddenly found out that I don't even belong to myself. I had to learn that my life isn't mine, it belongs to God. This was a big change in my life.

I love my ministry; it is a lot of work, but I love it. There is nothing better than witnessing someone else encounter God because you allowed yourself to be his instrument. For me there is no money or material possession in the universe that is better than that. At the end of the day, I understand and accept that I am not on this planet for myself; we are all here to serve and love one another as Jesus did.

—*Victor*

For Reflection

❋ Think of a time when someone served you. How did you feel? Humbled? Thankful? Loved? Draw inspiration from this experience and pray about ways you can help others feel the same. And always remember: "The first rule of ministry is serving someone other than yourself."

❋ In John's Gospel Jesus says, "I give you a new commandment, that you love one another. Just as I have loved you, you also should love one another" (Jn 13:34). God's love for us is pretty big. How can you develop that kind of love for others—including those you don't even know?

LOVE NO MATTER WHAT

Every year, my high school youth ministry group coordinates a one day retreat for each class. This year, I was asked to take on a larger part in the coordination. The first retreat I helped to coordinate was the Sophomore Retreat, "Love No Matter What."

The goal of the retreat was to bring everyone in the class together and focus on loving and supporting one another. The hope was that the retreat participants would focus on loving each other no matter the circumstance.

In my youth ministry program, I had learned to show my dedication and commitment to God and serve my brothers and sisters as he did. This retreat was a great opportunity for me and all the participants to get to know and understand some people we didn't associate with on a regular basis. Throughout the day, we were given the opportunity to comfort certain students. The students trustingly opened themselves up to us; it was a great blessing.

During this retreat I learned not to judge people until I know their story and even then, not to judge them at all. I learned to love and embrace others with kindness. Doing this made my life richer spiritually and I am very blessed to have had this opportunity.

—Paige

For Reflection

✹ Trying something new can sometimes be a bit intimidating, but it can also be an opportunity to have your horizons expanded. Reach out to one person who often seems to be on the margins.

✹ Recall a time when you were judged prematurely. How did it feel to have someone think they knew you without really getting to know you? Ask God to forgive those who judged you. Ask him for the grace to not judge others, but to find him in them.

GIVING THANKS

One of my earliest volunteering experiences stands out as an event that engaged me intellectually and morally. My mother used to work for the senior housing buildings in my town, and on Thanksgiving, when I was in sixth grade, it was her job to deliver turkey dinners to homebound seniors. My sister and I went along with her, and we delivered food to the elderly, who were incredibly grateful for both the dinners and our company. Many of the seniors told us how rarely they received visitors and how they were, therefore, frequently lonely. They loved having the simple opportunity to talk to us and tell us stories about their lives.

This experience taught me the value of service to others at a young age. I also became aware of the importance of personal interaction for all people. There are many people who do not receive the contact with others they need. Because of the example my parents gave me, I know how important it is to give even a little bit of time to show others that they are noticed and loved.

I love the personal interaction that service allows. So much of communication in today's world can be done through solitary means—like texting and instant messaging—that I appreciate the opportunities that community service provides for direct conversations with other people. It amazes me how much joy is brought to people simply by conversing with them and showing them that you care about them. I absolutely love seeing the look of profound appreciation when people in need are being assisted by others. Whether it be chatting with one of these senior housing residents, cheering on a runner at the Special Olympics, or doing landscaping for a home-bound person, the ability to communicate with and show love toward people is a blessing. Their happiness and thankfulness fills me with excitement and compels me to do more.

—*Owen*

For Reflection

✳ Loneliness can be very debilitating. What are some ways you can show others that they are not alone? How is God calling you to be part of someone else's life?

✳ This story speaks about solitary tasks such as texting and instant messages, but even these can be ways of witnessing to Christ. How can you use social media to accompany others in the way Jesus would want you to do?

PRAISING GOD TOGETHER

I have loved God and enjoyed helping others since a very young age. But when I turned twelve, I finally got the chance to help my mom and dad make food and distribute it to day laborers. These people stand on the street looking for work, they may not be in the country legally, may have minimal education, and barely make enough to support their families. With my family, I bring them a meal every week—and we also sing and praise God, giving them the spiritual motivation to not give up.

I love visiting these day laborers because I can relate to them in so many ways. I think about how blessed I am because, even though I, too, don't have my papers, I have been able to get an education. I also admire the stories they tell me because through them I learn that nothing is impossible.

Lastly, even though I am giving them a helping hand, they help me become more humble and courageous. I remember one time I went to do my normal routine making and distributing food with my mom and dad. We became overwhelmed with tears when, instead of us praying for the day laborers as was our custom, they prayed for us. I've been doing this with my family for five years and I still get the same feeling as the first time. God has opened my eyes through this ministry and I know God will continue to bless all who seek God's love.

—*Adan*

For Reflection

🌟 In John 21:15–19, Jesus asks Peter three times to "feed his sheep." Feeding a person can mean giving them food, but it can also mean nourishing them spiritually. What are some ways you can feed people who hunger for God?

🌟 We are all called to live in community and to care for one another. In community, we come together and share what we have and are nourished by the sharing. Think of three examples of how God has blessed you in the past twenty-four hours. How is God inviting you to share that blessing with others?

DIFFERENT

Each year I do Christian service with my school in Gardena, California. During my junior year, one particular service project caught my eye: the Special Olympics.

While I was there I talked with a teen who had ADHD (Attention Deficit Hyperactivity Disorder) and slight autism. I don't know why, but I had thought kids at Special Olympics would all *look* different. This teen I spoke to looked like a typical teen. When she asked me what Special Olympics team I played on, I let her know that I wasn't participating in the Special Olympics. I was there as a cheerleader and scorekeeper. She laughed and apologized. I asked her what made her think that I played on a Special Olympics team, and she told me that my inability to sit still made her think that I was like her. So I told her that I, too, have ADHD. She wondered aloud that I was normal and didn't have any noticeable physical disability.

I couldn't help but wonder why God makes everyone so different. And while wondering about those differences I realized that God still loves each of us. Being at the Special Olympics felt a little odd because I've never really been in a situation like that, but it also made me appreciate what it means to relate to someone who is different and not so different from me.

—*Kymieal*

For Reflection

✳ In Psalm 139 the psalmist reflects on the wonder that he is created by God. God knows us so well and nothing about us is secret from God. Pray with this psalm and thank God for creating you in love. Then think about others you know and thank God for creating them and loving them.

✳ Think of someone you know who you think is different from you. How is that person similar to you? Reflect on that person's gifts and how they could be used for God and his people.

KEEP THESE WORDS

Taking care of first- through third-grade children can really make me tired! My church is called Saint Mercurious and Saint Abraam Coptic Orthodox Church. Each year our church organizes a "Summer Camp" where kids of all ages can have fun, go on trips, and have times of prayer. Once you're a certain age, you can choose to become a junior chaperone—which is what I did last summer.

A junior chaperone is expected to take care of and bond with the group assigned to him or her. The group I was given had passed through several junior chaperones. They weren't cooperative, and they didn't want to listen to anyone. In fact, these young children thought of themselves as everyone else's boss. They looked innocent, but when it came to communicating with them, they didn't act that way. No chaperone wanted to deal with such a rambunctious group, and they were given to me.

Halfway through the summer, I was halfway through the hope that they would change. Some junior chaperones told me just to give up and pass them on to someone else. That's when it hit me. These kids weren't close to God; they weren't experiencing God's love during camp. Each day we had a thirty-minute lesson which usually was an open discussion. One day I chose to read and discuss Deuteronomy 6: 4–9:

> Hear, O Israel: The LORD is our God, the LORD alone. You shall love the LORD your God with all your heart, and with all your soul, and with all your might. Keep these words that I am commanding you today in your heart. Recite them to your children and talk about them when you are at home and when you are away, when you lie down and when you rise. Bind them as a sign on your hand, fix them as an emblem on your forehead, and write them on the doorposts of your house and on your gates.

I chose this citation because it relates to obedience. I really felt God helping me while we were discussing this; God was with me. The kids seemed . . .

obedient. I believe that God gave me the ability to talk with them. I had them memorize, "Keep these words that I am commanding you today in your heart." After this lesson, I heard them repeating this verse and then listening to the other chaperones. They were acting as innocent as their faces looked.

I was thanked a lot. I couldn't help but think that they should have been thanking God instead. God gave me the strength, patience, and intuition to help my group of kids. He worked through me, and I'm glad that he did. I could have given up, but I didn't, and God was with me. I look back at this experience and say *Noshkar Rabena*, "Thank you, God" in Arabic.

—*Kathryn*

For Reflection

✷ One of the ways that God chooses to speak to us is through Scripture. Re-read the passage from Deuteronomy. What word or phrase stands out for you? What do you think God is challenging you to do with that phrase?

✷ In this story, the young children had trouble being obedient. The author was being asked for her own obedience to the call to serve the kids. When have you had trouble sticking to something that was hard to do? What made it possible for you to follow through?

CALLED AND CHOSEN

The summer I went on a retreat in Hemet, California, was when my relationship with God grew stronger. The retreat's theme was, "Called and Chosen." It gave us, the participants, time to learn to work together, to get closer to God, and to understand ourselves better so that we could return to our high school and be leaders of our school community.

Before the retreat, there was a lot going on in my life. During the retreat we had prayer walks, adoration, and time just to talk to God. This time with God helped me realize that he can wash away all my worries. I opened my heart to him, and that was the best thing I have ever done. I experienced God calling me to be his child, his disciple, and a leader to my peers by spreading his word and telling them about God's amazing love for them. I also learned that in order to lead others, first I must follow Christ myself.

Before going on the retreat I thought I was already the closest I could be with the Lord, but being on that retreat changed my life in so many ways. I learned that a part of living my own life includes having God in it because he wants me to love him and share the life he gave me with him. I am forever grateful that God helped me come to that realization.

—Alea

For Reflection

✷ "In order to lead others, first I must follow Christ myself." A disciple cannot give what he or she does not have. Before, during, and after serving our brothers and sisters in Christ, we must be nourished by Christ so as to give him to others. Although your day may be full, take some time—even just fifteen minutes—to be with God by either going on a prayer walk (walking in a quiet, recollected manner while praying or talking to God), praying before the Blessed Sacrament, or reflecting on a Scripture passage. Allow God to fill you so that you can bring him to others.

✷ Jesus was a leader who came "among [us] as one who serves" (Lk 22:27). Think about a role in which you are a leader—at school, on a team, in an activity, or even just being an older sibling. How can service become leadership for you? How can leadership become service?

TAKING NOTHING FOR GRANTED

This summer, I went on a service trip to Camden, New Jersey, with my youth group from St. Ignatius Parish. I had heard inspiring stories from those who had gone in previous years, and I wanted to be a part of that myself. For five days, our group volunteered at nursing homes, pre-schools, and homeless shelters. Some of my good friends and I were placed at Genesis, a nursing home. We helped the nurses throughout the day by serving coffee, doing crafts, and playing games with the elderly.

Vince, one of the men at Genesis, had a particular impact on me. He resided on the floor where I spent most of my time, the Alzheimer's floor. Most of the residents on this floor were at least seventy years old, but Vince was only fifty-six. He would walk around with a binder full of pictures, muttering jumbled words to himself. One morning, we played a modified version of mini golf with the patients, and Vince, eager to win, was really getting into the game. When he won by a good fifty points, the smile on Vince's face lit up the room. His smile made me realize that it's the little things in life that matter the most. I also discovered I enjoy other people's happiness as much as my own.

Every time I saw a resident at Genesis smile, I was reminded that even though these people are in the last years of their lives, God is with them every day. I saw that the elderly in this nursing home did not have much, and I became even more grateful for the things I have. At times during this trip, I would realize how fortunate I am to live in a safe community with opportunities given to me left and right. I have learned to be grateful for everything I have and to take nothing for granted.

—Luisa

For Reflection

✳ In this story, Luisa realizes that "it's the little things in life that matter most." Even Jesus talks about doing little things for love of him (Mt 25:40). What little things can you do today to love God and others? By loving those around us in big and little ways, we are loving God!

✳ Who do you love? What have you done to show the people around you today that you love them? What are some small things you could do to show love at home, in school, at church?

SPECIAL OLYMPICS

Through my high school youth program, LIFE Team, I attended a volunteer service project with the Special Olympics. The Special Olympics is an organization that provides children and adults with intellectual disabilities year-round sports training and competitions in Olympic-type sports. I was assigned to help with a few different things, but my favorite was being in charge of small games for the competitors to play. Every time I saw them play the mini games, I could see a light of happiness come from their eyes, and it grew even brighter when they won a prize. From early morning to late afternoon, I was able to bring joy to adults and children with special needs; and their joy gave me joy.

God told us to go out into the world to serve others and to give everything to those who need it. As I was helping, I remembered Acts 20:35, "In all this I have given you an example that by such work we must support the weak, remembering the words of the Lord Jesus, for he himself said, 'It is more blessed to give than to receive.'"

As members of our group were leaving, not only was the staff of the Special Olympics thankful, but the adults and children were, too. Through this experience God not only strengthened my faith, he also gave me deep joy.

—*Luis*

For Reflection

✳ *"The joy of the LORD is your strength"* (Neh 8:10). Joy is a great sign of faith. What things bring you joy? How can you share this joy with others?

✳ Happiness is contagious. Do something that makes someone smile and laugh. See how he or she responds and how your attitude changes, too!

PUPPETEERS FOR CHRIST

In middle and high school, I participated in a club my mom started in my homeschool group. The group's purpose was to teach young children about God. Under my mom's direction, a group of my friends and I made puppets and wrote plays to teach children about Jesus. We called ourselves the 11th Commandment Puppeteers, inspired by Jesus's final command to his disciples, "Go therefore and make disciples of all the nations" (Mt 28:19). We wanted to do what Jesus said and spread God's message of love in a creative way.

After a year of making the puppets, writing and editing scripts, memorizing lines, and collecting props, our small group was ready to visit a local preschool. Armed with a PVC pipe theater, plastic bins full of puppets, and wearing black t-shirts to blend with the backdrop, we faced a room of about twenty preschoolers. We were ready to share God's

Good News with them. The shows had themes such as obedience, generosity, trust in the Lord, and using our talents for God. At first we performed them for preschoolers in religious education classes. Later we also performed for the elderly in nursing homes and senior citizen centers.

Though the plays were written in a simple style with young children in mind, I learned from them as well. Repeating the messages every few weeks in the shows truly ingrained them into my mind, so I not only knew Jesus's teachings—I also lived them. Even the preschool songs that were stuck in my head echoed God's word. I grew in my own faith by teaching it in a simple manner. Much can be learned from simplicity. Saint Thérèse of Lisieux said that our Lord needs from us neither great deeds, nor profound thoughts. Neither intelligence nor talents. He cherishes simplicity.

—*Kathleen*

For Reflection

✳ What does it mean to be a disciple of God? How is God asking you to live your discipleship?

✳ Simplicity can bring greater clarity to situations. Is there some tangible way you can simplify at least one thing in your life today? How can you bring this about and what do you think the result will be?

MISSION TO THE MILITARY

For my Eagle Scout project I decided to make and send care packages overseas to our men and women serving in the Armed Forces. After contacting the United Service Organization (USO) in Jacksonville, Florida, I had a list of items to put into the packages. The USO recommended that I fill the boxes with the kinds of things people normally have around the house, the kinds of things we take for granted.

I made copies of the list to hand out to people, and my church's bulletin placed an announcement about collecting the items. I was also able to put a box in my church for people to place their donations. Even the Cub Scouts and a summer Band Camp helped collect items. After a month and a half of collecting, I got the flat rate boxes the packages would be shipped in. With my fellow Boy Scouts, we filled sixty-six boxes with care packages that my parents and I took to the USO.

There were many people other than me who made this delivery of care packages possible: my parents, troop leaders, other scouts, parishioners of my church, and the USO. I am proud to have been able to show our military personnel in this small way how much people appreciate their service. May God bless them always!

—Benjamin

For Reflection

✳ What items do you have around your house that you take for granted? Do you take the time to realize that everything you have comes from the grace of God?

✳ Who helps you to make your accomplishments possible? How can you show your gratitude to these people?

THE MONDAY MORNING CREW

Every Monday morning, thirty to eighty people gather on the sidewalk outside of an abortion clinic in Maryland for peaceful prayer and protest. They are the "Monday Morning Crew," and they pray for women who find themselves unsure about what to do after becoming pregnant.

One summer I decided to join them for an hour a week. Since some of my family and friends also went, it became a sort of social gathering as well as a time for intense prayer. By praying rosaries and holding signs, we were able to witness to our faith while hanging out together.

At first I didn't think too deeply about what was happening behind the doors of the clinic. Then, in late August, it hit close to home. I was standing and holding signs with my brothers near the entrance to the business complex. As I watched cars drive in and out I suddenly saw a familiar face.

"*NO!*" I thought to myself as I dropped my sign and followed the car from a distance. I recognized the seventeen-year-old girl in the passenger seat and her boyfriend at the wheel; they went to my high school. My mind raced, "*Maybe they're just going to the dentist . . .*" My hope was quickly broken when the car pulled up right in front of the abortion clinic.

I could have said something—anything—to make them turn around. There was a thirty-second window of opportunity from when they exited the car to when they entered the clinic. I could have shouted out her name. I could have said she didn't have to do it . . . but I stayed silent. Then the clinic escorts quickly ushered the couple straight into the clinic. Just like that, my window of opportunity slammed shut.

Sometimes I still wonder if that day really happened. Maybe I had imagined it. But I didn't. If I had imagined it, I would not have asked every person outside the clinic that day to pray for my classmates. If I had imagined it, I would not have worn my pro-life t-shirt every Monday in school the following year. If I had imagined it, I would not have given a week-long series of talks on abortion to my school's Bible study club. If I had imagined it, I would not be thinking and praying about a religious vocation with the Sisters of Life.

The thing is, I wasn't even supposed to be at the clinic that day. I was supposed to be babysitting. But God had other plans for me. God always has a plan, even if it isn't *my* plan.

—*Mary*

For Reflection

✳ Sometimes when we manage to respond to a difficult situation with a positive attitude, we begin to see God's plan in it. Maybe you, a friend, or a family member is going through a difficult time. How might the Lord be asking you to love in this situation?

✳ Have you seen God use the difficult experiences in your life for your benefit and for the benefit of others? Pray for the grace of perseverance and courage, knowing that Jesus is "with you always" (Mt 28:20).

CITY OF BOYS

I was part of a mission team that went to Cusco, Peru, for two weeks to work with the Missionary Servants of the Poor of the Third World. Together, we twelve boys and seven girls went outside our comfort zones to honor and trust God by working with our brothers and sisters in Christ.

The boys' team worked at the City of Boys. This is a place where priests give boys from ages seven to eighteen a basic education, teach them the faith, and help them to learn skills that can help them live in Peru. These skills include pottery, gardening, cheese making, and woodworking.

The volunteer work at the City of Boys involved two big construction projects. After work was done for the day, we would play soccer, football, or rugby with the Peruvian boys.

One day after Mass we went to a poor village. There I saw kids under ten years old gleaning corn to earn their lunch because their parents were too poor to feed them. Many of the kids' clothes were torn and dirty. When they had time to play, they rolled a rusty wheel around or played volleyball with a ripped-up ball.

The experiences God gave me caused me to realize how ungrateful I had been for most things in my life. I saw how I often wanted more and more, while my brothers and sisters in Christ were in need of so much. It's hard to put into words how I feel about the poor now. I plan to devote more time to them and less time thinking about myself.

—Patrick

For Reflection

✳ Read about Saint Paul's conversion in Acts 9:1–19. We all need reminders to change our old ways of thinking and turn our hearts to Christ. Sometimes it can be a dramatic moment like with Saint Paul; other times, God works more subtly. Have you had a turning point in your life? If so, what was it? How did it change your point of view?

✳ Often those we serve can remind us that we are called to give thanks to God with grateful hearts. Before going to sleep, tell God five things you are thankful for that day. Then think about one area you fell short in. Ask for his forgiveness and guidance to do better tomorrow. Consider making this a nightly practice.

"HOPE DOES NOT DISAPPOINT"

Twice during high school, I took part in mission trips with my parish youth group living and working at an orphanage for disabled children in Nicaragua. Both times our trip consisted of more than simply digging foundations or mixing cement (which we did a lot of); the trips were life-changing experiences that revolutionized my perspective on the world. The greatest lesson I learned was also the simplest: With God, there is always joy and hope.

The children of this orphanage were the most vulnerable and marginalized in society: orphans with disabilities living in a poverty-stricken, developing country. Yet, these same children were the most joyful individuals I had ever met. We would play, dance, and laugh with them constantly, and it brought us overwhelming fulfillment to know that just our presence was able to put a smile on their faces and bring them joy.

My second trip was two years after my first. A lot had changed: there was now another dormitory house, an administration/classroom building, and a chapel under construction on the property. There were also several more children living in the orphanage. It was amazing to see how the work of many missionaries had built up this community, and I was happy to have been a part of it. This place gives hope to these kids, who, without this orphanage, might be in even more harmful situations.

The most important thing, I kept reminding myself, was that it was not us doing these things; it was God working through us. Although living in an orphanage is far from the ideal living condition or situation for any child, God working through people makes it possible for these children to smile and receive at least some of what they need. It is through God that both they, and we, experience joy and hope, and "hope does not disappoint" (Rom 5:5).

—Shane

For Reflection

✳ Though young, the children the author met had great strength, hope, and joy in the face of adversity. When you are troubled, where do you go to seek consolation? When others need help, do they know they can find it in you?

✳ Sometimes it can take a long time to see the fruits of our labors; so long that it might be hard to believe that one small project—like mixing cement—can transform lives. Reflect on a project, service, or task you contributed only a part to. Thank God for the contributions of others and ask him to continue to bless those who were helped.

THE MISSION OF ACCOMPANIMENT

The first time I went to a home for the elderly with my school group I didn't know what to expect. At other community service locations, tasks are straightforward: packing boxes of food or clothes, giving hot meals to the homeless or hungry persons, etc. At the home for the elderly, our "task" was to visit the residents and accompany them for a couple of hours.

Although I was scared on my first day, my first look at Clark House calmed me. It's a beautiful place with a large, newly constructed white building and brightly colored floral arrangements enhancing the grounds. Once in the lobby, our school group was directed to a patio where aides had wheeled out several elderly men and women—people who rarely had anyone visit them. We visited with the residents and talked with them. This was a challenge since most of the residents had lost some of their hearing, memory, or ability to talk. Conversations with them could be discouraging, especially if you expected answers to all of your questions.

With time, however, I learned to accept the residents' limitations and recognize how much they really appreciated the company. Regardless of whether they could answer my questions, hear what I said, or even acknowledge my presence, they seemed happy to have company. For me, the best thing about visiting Clark House was seeing the smiles on the people's faces as they simply looked at us. Without saying a single word they communicated how much they appreciated the time we took to be with them.

—Cecily

For Reflection

✴ Sometimes, serving others involves something to do: clear tasks with directions and an objective. But often service is just about presence. Some of Jesus's greatest acts were just in being with a person. Look up the corporal and spiritual works of mercy. Two are to visit the sick and comfort the afflicted. Choose one and see how being the gift of presence is an act of service.

✴ Understanding is central to communication; it can be extraordinarily difficult to reach someone when you are unable to communicate or do not speak the same language. And yet the residents in the story understood that the author and others were communicating love. What are some ways you can bring God's love to those who cannot hear or see or simply don't speak the same language?

SERVING THROUGH SONG

Well, at first I didn't know exactly what to expect of any Christian ministry and really couldn't see myself doing any type of service for anyone. I had always been involved in my church, but I just wasn't a service type of person.

Then one day I was asked to help during adoration of the Blessed Sacrament and Mass. I always enjoyed singing, but it had never occurred to me that I could use my voice in service. At first, I was really shy.

In time, I began to understand that God gave me a talent for singing, and it was a talent that I could use in serving him and others. Whenever I sing during Mass or adoration my heart is filled with the Holy Spirit. I can bring others to worship and talk to Jesus by doing what I love.

There has been some negativity thrown at me for serving as a music minister. Some students put me down, call me names, and make fun of me. But none of that has stopped me. Singing isn't about me or the other students; it's about me ministering to the students and serving God with the gift he has given me. Now, I realize that everything I do, especially when I'm singing in church, I do for the Lord.

—Emerald

For Reflection

✳ "You are the light of the world. A city built on a hill cannot be hid. No one after lighting a lamp puts it under the bushel basket, but on the lampstand, and it gives light to all in the house. In the same way, let your light shine before others, so that they may see your good works and give glory to your Father in heaven." (Mt 5:14–16)

What talent or gift do you have that you are reluctant to share with others? How could God be asking you to share that gift with others?

✳ Have you ever been teased when you did something for another person? Have you ever teased someone else when they were helping another person? Pray for those who have teased you and ask God to forgive you for having teased another.

LIFTING SPIRITS AND GIVING THANKS

As I greeted each section of the homeless and underprivileged men, women, and children of the Washington, D.C., area, I was reminded of the great blessing my Lord has bestowed on me.

Recently, I was able to volunteer at Christ House, an organization that hosts dinners and provides shelter for people that need help getting back on their feet after a crisis. It is a blessing to be a part of groups like these.

One Friday afternoon I went to Christ House with a group from school. We had prepared food, served it, and then just spent time with the people there. As I listened to their stories, a great sense of sadness came over me, and I felt sympathy for the difficulties they had been through. Then I remembered why I was there: to help as much I could, to listen, and to remind them that they can trust God. I could feel that God's presence was with us and that he saw and heard us.

When I look back at this experience I think of the memorable people I encountered and helped. I am also reminded of the great privileges I have in my life. I thank my Lord every single day for the many blessings in my life.

—*Rosie*

For Reflection

✳ When you serve others who are less fortunate than yourself, you might feel sadness and sympathy—be humbled by your blessings, or guilty that you've taken them for granted. How can you refocus your spirit so that your service concentrates on the person you are serving and not yourself?

✳ Jesus was a great listener. People often came to him with their stories and needs. Pray about doing some volunteer or service work that will bring you into contact with people who have stories to share. Ask Jesus to help you listen as he did, and then extend his mercy to the person you are listening to.

TIRING, TOUGH, AND WORTH IT

I completed my junior year service work with the Holy Name Youth Service Project in West Roxbury. After a lot of local service projects and fund raisers, we went on a service trip to New Orleans to help those who, so many years later, are still trying to recuperate from Hurricane Katrina.

Our work was tiring and tough, but it was definitely worth every second. We cleaned trashed lots, painted houses, took down fences, built fences, and helped kids with homework in an after-school program. The residents were amazing—they welcomed us as if we were family, and we couldn't have been more grateful for all they did for us.

Coming into this service trip, I was a lukewarm Catholic, but in just a short period of time I was closer to God than I had ever been. My service work in New Orleans has left me wanting more. I cannot wait to go back so I can continue what my group started. Volunteer service and the people I have met have changed my life, and now I feel a desire to help change others' lives.

—*Brendan*

For Reflection

✹ Brendan's story shows the power of service even in small ways, and how that can bring you closer to God. How may God be calling you to serve those in your community and in your church? In what ways will it bring *you* closer?

✹ Look up the prayer "Christ Has No Body" by Saint Teresa of Avila. Read it once focusing on how it references your body. What do your eyes show him? Where do your feet take you to do good? Then read it again, this time meditating on how the prayer could refer to the body of the Church—everyone together. Identify a need in your community or elsewhere. How can you and the people in your life work to be Christ?

DOING WHAT JESUS WOULD DO

Volunteering reinforces a key Christian virtue: helping others. I am constantly reminded to care for others as the great community servant, Jesus Christ, did. Volunteering allows me to use my time productively and to be the best person I can be. Seeing so many people less fortunate than I has reminded me how blessed I am to have everything I need. It also makes me realize how unjust it would be not to share my time and abilities with others who need assistance in some way.

The summer of eighth grade, I did a week of volunteering with my church. We helped out at a different location each day of the week. From nursing homes to donation centers—the common element in each experience was that we were doing what Jesus would do when he encountered someone in need.

My favorite event was on the last day, Friday, when we served dinner at the Pine Street Inn—a homeless shelter offering food, shelter, and job training—in Boston. The many people that came through the line as I passed out dessert varied in age, physical appearance, and disposition. It proved to me and to all of us there that there is no one type of person who is homeless; any person can be a person without shelter.

My volunteer work has inspired me to seek a career centered on helping others. I'm so appreciative that my parents have instilled the value of service in me, and I know that I will continue to serve the community and God throughout my life.

—*Owen*

For Reflection

✳ While people who are poor, homeless, or ill are almost invisible to society, celebrities cannot go anywhere without people noticing them. Yet, Jesus identifies himself with the poor and marginalized of society. Imagine that you saw Jesus dressed in rags holding an empty cup begging for money. How would you respond? How would your response be not just a blessing for the person begging but a blessing for you?

✳ The author brings up the concept of justice. What does justice mean to you? How can your service and mission be a form of justice?

FEELING MISSION

My father has been a leader of a youth group since I was two years old. Because of that, I grew up knowing people that loved, praised, and adored God. As I grew, I came to know God for myself. When I went to high school I got up early on Saturday mornings, but it wasn't to watch TV. Instead, I joined classmates and peers from the youth group on service projects.

Volunteering on service projects wasn't and isn't always an easy task. It's a sacrifice—prayer nights, Mass, adoration, retreats, and work all take time. But these things are all worthwhile. For example, after one of the testimonies I was asked to give at a retreat, a girl told me I had changed her way of thinking about things. It was humbling. In that moment I felt mission—a mission not to serve myself but that others may better know our Lord and love him like I do.

—*Asalia*

For Reflection

✳ What do you think it means to "feel" mission? How would you translate those feelings into actions?

✳ When we sacrifice, we have to give up something: time, money, favorite food, or activity. Mission involves sacrifice. Is there something you could give up that would help you on the mission God calls you to?

BEING WHO GOD CREATED ME TO BE

I went on a service trip to New Orleans to help people who are still affected from the destruction left by Hurricane Katrina. Our group served at a variety of places. We cleaned trashed lots—where many illicit activities allegedly took place—worked on houses that needed fixing or maintenance, and helped at after school programs. I thought I would be working the whole time and that the work would make me miserable. I was right . . . I did work all the time. But I was also wrong; I was hardly miserable.

It is hard to be miserable while being around such amazing people. The people were awesome, funny, and all-around good. At one point in the week we were all sitting around making small talk with one another. I was just being myself and I realized how much things had changed from the beginning of the week. It is mind-blowing to me that we all became such good friends. I had expected to make two or three new friends, but I never expected them to accept me as I am. They became my family away from home; they kept me going and showed me what is possible when you work together. This experience made me so happy that I could barely control myself. Self-confidence has never been my strong suit, and now, thanks to this trip, I'm bursting with it!

I learned so much in the midst of all the hard work. I learned that people are better than I had given them credit for. I learned to be myself—because before this I would hold back my full personality and just tried to fit in with the crowd. Now I can be happy with who I am and not be afraid to show myself to others. In a nutshell, I learned the importance of both being myself and accepting others for who they are.

—*Brendan*

For Reflection

✴ We are all called to serve Christ. Think back to a time or place where you have served. Now put yourself in the opposite role, and think about what it would have been like to receive the service you gave. Christ did the same sort of role reversal by coming to the earth as a meek and humble human.

✴ Prejudice can be a pretty hard thing to overcome. Sometimes we think we know how something will turn out. How does going into a situation with a negative mindset affect the situation? What can you do to remain positive and open to new people and experiences?

OVERCOMING NERVES

A typical hot and humid June day greeted me the morning I left for a service work camp. The only reason I went was because my friend's father had called my dad and asked if I could accompany his daughter at service work camp. The two of them thought it was a good idea. I wasn't so sure I did.

There were a lot of unknowns. The only thing I really knew was that I would be spending a week helping the needy make their homes more suitable. This was as far as my knowledge went; the rest was truly new territory. Leaving my family to go to the Arlington Diocese service work camp for a week with absolutely no modern communications technology made me even more wary. I didn't leave for my grand adventure alone; joining me was an old friend: nervous anxiety.

Every morning of service work camp began with Mass, and each day ended in prayer. This gave us a constant reminder that God's will was our ultimate goal. That affected how we experienced our daily duties at the work sites. Lunch conversations often centered on the effectiveness of God's great hand in our own lives, and the difficulties and joys of being a young, active Catholic in a world that doesn't often promote or support a culture of faith.

We worked hard, but we also had a lot of fun. Water bottle fights, using funny accents while speaking, songs echoing in the small room when painting, piggy back rides, and pranks among the work groups—laughter and diligence went together. The fun also helped to combat homesickness and made the week go by at top speed. In the process all my anxieties disappeared and I was able to really enjoy myself. At service work camp I learned that by doing God's will I can be truly satisfied. God is good.

—*Julia Marie*

For Reflection

✺ Take time to disconnect for a few minutes like they did in the camp. Allow the peace of Christ to fill you. This is a moment for Christ and you.

✺ We all have to do things we don't like doing. Sometimes just showing up is part of the battle. But if we trust in God, he will help us get through the job. Ask God to help you feel satisfied doing something you dread. Offer the task to God as a sacrifice for someone else.

THE REAL WORLD

This past summer I went on a service trip with members of my church's youth community to Camden, New Jersey. We stayed at the Romero Center, which is an organization that facilitates service trips incorporating into their mission Archbishop Oscar Romero's philosophy on social justice issues. On the first night of the trip, we were placed into groups of four from the various organizations visiting the Romero Center for that week. These groups of four were affectionately called "families." To better understand what the people in the area live every day we were given $3 each or a family total of $12. We were told to use that money to buy food for our three meals for the next day. This amount represented what Camden residents living on food stamps would receive for a given day: $3 a person.

When we were first given the assignment, I thought the greatest challenge would be to buy enough food to sustain the four of us for a whole twenty-four hours. However, upon arriving at the grocery store, I quickly realized that the food itself was rather insignificant; the real challenge was being thrown into "real-world" Camden.

As soon as we entered the grocery store we stood out. There we were—a group of about fifty white high school kids—on a kind of "scavenger hunt." But our game was the everyday existence for the other people in the store. Realizing that was a humbling wake-up call. I began to understand what it was like to live in poverty, to appreciate how truly blessed I am, and perhaps most significantly to gain a real sense of solidarity with people who are our brothers and sisters in Christ.

—Grace H.

For Reflection

✽ Oscar Romero was Archbishop of San Salvador, El Salvador, from 1977–1980. He spoke out about the injustices the poor people of his country were experiencing at the hands of those in power. Because of his defense of the rights of the marginalized he was assassinated. Sadly, there are many places in our world where people daily suffer grave injustices. How can you respond to their needs where you live?

✽ To be in solidarity with someone does not necessarily mean moving and living the other's reality daily. What are some ways you can live in solidarity with those who suffer?

DOING THE RIGHT THING

It was not the first time I had ever done service; however, it was the first time that I reflected on what I was actually doing.

Last year, when I was a sophomore, I signed up to help Habitat for Humanity over spring break. As part of that team, I helped break down, clean up, and make a house livable for a family in need.

I was surprised that throughout the day I never once wondered, *"How much longer do I need to be here?"* Not once did I wish the day would just be over. Instead, I really enjoyed working with the other students and volunteers from Habitat for Humanity. We came together with the same mind: to accomplish a task. Even though we did not know one another well, over the hours of working together we grew to be friends.

Helping a family in need to get back on their feet with a place to live was a humbling experience. It felt good to help others. The fact that I did not know the family made the project have more of an impact for me. Not knowing them and not feeling obligated to help allowed me to see that I could help someone out of the kindness of my heart, and not expect anything in return. Since that day, I have really enjoyed doing Christian service. I realize how it benefits others and I feel happy knowing that I am doing the right thing.

—Adoree'

For Reflection

✳ It's hard to stay focused. What thoughts and distractions go through your mind when you're doing an act of service—whether it be with a project, time spent with others, or even a chore at home? What are some things you can do to become more fully present in what you're doing?

✳ Have you been living your life on autopilot, not really taking stock on what impact (good or bad) your words and actions have? Go back to a time when you may have done something good without really thinking about it. How do you think your words or actions may have impacted others in a meaningful way?

WHY I SAY "Y'ALL"

As a little girl, I was somewhat reckless and quite impatient—traits that resulted in an inordinate amount of scrapes and scabs, and a tendency to tear them open before they were healed. I never minded. To me, they seemed almost like bold reminders of a trial by fire akin to a soldier's wounds, the small pain that came with them proof of battle—or, more likely, proof that I lived.

In reality, there are physical wounds and there are wounds of the heart. Everyone has a wound emblazoned somewhere on his or her soul. The wound could be the loss of someone dear—one that, with time, holds not just grief, but the joyful memory of the person. Or it could be an experience that touches the heart so deeply that one would never wish to recover from it. That's what my mission experience in Tuscaloosa, Alabama, is for me.

That July I ended up with forty people I barely knew, mostly high school students like me, on a trip sponsored by the archdiocesan Office for Youth Ministry. The Gospel Road II program was a service and poverty encounter experience. Like my soon-to-be-friends, I was unsure what to expect. I hadn't traveled to many southern states before. Being a fan of accents and dialects, however, I hoped to pick up a bit of Alabama's southern drawl. Most specifically, I wanted to learn how to say "y'all" just right. Perhaps it was because I like country music, or because in a random flight of fancy I'd decided it was definitely one of the best accents to emulate. I had it all planned—I'd fit in perfectly with my acquired "y'all."

Holy Spirit Parish in Tuscaloosa welcomed us with unmatched graciousness. But I should have known myself well enough to realize that once I got there, I wouldn't dare speak the way the locals did—it was pretentious, right? I wasn't from the South, I wasn't staying, and when it came down to it, I had no real right to say "y'all." It didn't really belong to me.

Our group traveled around—painting houses, doing yard work, visiting, even laying down linoleum (a little jagged around the edges, I must admit). We came back to a church whose parishioners cooked for us every night and had Krispy Kreme donuts every morning. And somehow, as much as I refused to allow myself to speak with a southern accent, I found myself wanting to be like them.

At the time I didn't know what it was exactly that attracted me to the people there, what made me so want to be like them. Now, with time and space between us, I realize it was the generosity of their community. I'd never really seen that kind of openness before. It's just not done up North where I grew up. Sure, we have food drives and clothing drives and we care about others, but the people in Tuscaloosa welcomed us into their homes, cooked for us, and served us every night. We didn't ask them to do it, but then—as far as they were concerned—we didn't have to. They saw us as their guests—with sleeping bags in their preschool rooms and over half the church hall. It didn't matter to them that the whole reason we were there was to serve—not be served. The greatest gift I received from them was learning how to receive what they offered graciously.

I can't help but be reminded of the story of the widow's mite in which Jesus chastises those who give from their abundance, and exalts one woman who gives all she had, little though it may have seemed.

Holy Spirit Parish is not a wealthy community, but it is a blessed one. The spirit of generosity and Southern hospitality is a richness that flooded us all. Red and Leroy, who had only a trailer and a small plot of land for subsistence farming, shared all they had with us, even their meager food supply. There were also some nuns from Italy there who gave us drinks and ice cream—even though it must've cost them dearly to do that for forty kids three days in a row. Time and again we witnessed this generosity of spirit.

I left Alabama wanting to be like the people I met there; in fact, I still do. By the end of the trip I was unable to stop myself from slipping into Southern phrases, but couldn't help saying "you all." I was very silly. People so generous could not mind sharing their accent with a fifteen-year-old from Boston. A chaperone from Mississippi finally heard my awkward "you all" along with some others' attempts to avoid drawl, and she had laughter in her eyes as she teased, "Come on, folks, it's 'y'all.'" I finally began to say it.

Most of us came back saying "y'all," but I believe I am the only one who still does. There are other ways to keep the soul-wound from Alabama open,

I imagine. But for me, every time I say "y'all," I still think of Tuscaloosa and Greene County, Eutaw and Boligee. I still think of forty kids from Boston trying to love as God taught us. I still think of sugary Krispy Kreme and "sweet tea" that seemed bitter and all those wonderful, gut-wrenching days. I don't have a bandage or scar that points to this wound; I have only my heart and my memory and my own duty to keep my memories of that time fresh. So I say "y'all," and guard against the day I would stop and close the wound that the love I experienced in Alabama gave me. God help me if I ever stop, for that will be the day I have forgotten why I say "y'all," and how I came to say it in the first place.

—*Alice*

For Reflection

✳ We usually think of a wound as something that hurts and needs to be healed. To the apostle Thomas, however, wounds were proof—hard evidence that the person standing before him was Jesus, risen from the dead. Soul wounds also show us Christ, both in bearing them and exposing them. Have you ever felt "wounded" in this way? What would it take for something to touch you that deeply?

✳ Alice was most touched by the generosity of the people she served and realized that you don't need to have much in order to give much. What do you have little of? Time, energy, money, spirit? How can you be generous with what you do have?

WORKS AND BLESSINGS OF GOD

Being a part of campus ministry at my high school has opened my eyes to the works and blessings of God. It has also made me feel comfortable expressing my faith to others.

One of the best things about campus ministry is the people I get to experience my faith journey with. I have had the chance to make amazing friendships, friendships based on shared faith and the love of Christ. Whenever I am having a bad day, the others instantly know there is something wrong and try their best to comfort me. Because we have come to know each other so well, we can be there to rejoice or support one another. These are friendships I believe will last a lifetime.

Being able to spread the Good News in a relatable way to other students my age is an amazing experience. One specific way I am able to do this is by being a Life Night coordinator at my school.

During Life Night we focus on a specific topic along with praise and worship. We usually have a student announce the theme and explain how that topic relates to them. Although I am still learning more about Christ and my faith every day, this experience has given me the ability to reach others by sharing my experiences of God at work in my life.

I am forever grateful for this experience and hope that all teenagers accept any opportunity to hear the word of God.

—*Veronica K.*

For Reflection

✳ How do others bring Christ to you in word and action?

✳ If you were asked to present a specific theme related to your faith, what would you want to present? How would you prepare for this? What would you choose to share? What would you choose to remain private?

SIMPLY HAPPY

Because I love kids and horses, my best friend—who is also my sister—and I have volunteered every Monday for the past three years at a therapeutic riding stable that helps kids with physical disabilities. It may sound kind of weird, but it's actually really cool. The horses' motions help the kids to stretch and strengthen their muscles.

When I first started helping at the stable I was kind of sad to see so many kids with leg braces, crutches, and wheelchairs. I thought, "*Why would God do this to someone?*" But once I started working with them, I realized that these kids are happy to be alive—they weren't sad. They don't care that they aren't like other kids; they are just happy to be themselves. I also realized how much joy they bring into their parents' and siblings' lives. It was wonderful to be with a smiling kid as they waited for a horse to ride. These kids are a blessing to their families and to me!

In the end, the "why" someone is a certain way isn't something I need to concern myself with. What matters most is the person. God showed me that it doesn't matter if people are different, how they look, or what they can or cannot do. The kids are amazing—they don't look in a mirror and say, "Oh, I don't like my hair or my eyes"; they are happy. Just simply happy. I am amazed how volunteering has made me feel close to God and these kids. This was and is one of the best experiences of my life.

—Catherine

For Reflection

✳ No one's perfect. What kinds of internal or external challenges or limitations do you have? How can those things also be part of a person's witness to God's work in their lives? How can your limitations still speak to others about your relationship with God?

✳ Who is a blessing in your life and why? What are your strengths? What are your limitations? How can you be a greater blessing to others?

A WHOLE NEW LIGHT

I was a practicing Catholic teenager. I went to Mass on Sundays, went to confession once or twice a month, and attended every youth conference that came along. Then, a few years ago, I heard a priest from the Missionary Servants of the Poor of the Third World talk in Buffalo, New York. What I heard changed my life.

The priest spoke about the work his missionary order does for God in the Andes Mountains in Cusco, Peru. I was hooked, and later—after a lot of fundraising—I was able to join a group from Buffalo for a two-week mission experience.

When we arrived, we were given a tour of where we would be living and then got to work. We helped shovel dirt and rocks in the mornings to make new stables for the cows and some shower stalls. In the afternoons, we helped kids with school work and played sports with them.

At night we spent an hour in adoration before the Blessed Sacrament and prayed compline—the Church's night prayer. Listening to the beautiful voices of the young local seminarians singing in Spanish and Latin in the adoration chapel and feeling close to God while serving the poor completely changed my spiritual life.

My experiences in Peru made my problems seem so little and insignificant. I felt so on fire with love for God that it put everything else in a whole new light. I realized that it's not so hard to put aside my troubles and follow the path that God set for me.

—*Richard*

For Reflection

✳ Prior to the trip the author was doing everything the Church asks and more, but it took this trip to light him on fire with the Holy Spirit. Are there some ways in which practicing your faith is just going through the motions? What can you do to light the fire in yourself?

✳ Do you remember the greatness of God in comparison to your problems? What difficulties are you facing? Speak to God about them and entrust yourself to him and his deep love for you.

TEACHING AND LEADING

I have enjoyed teaching religious education classes for the past three years. I have worked with elementary, middle, and high school students. All of these experiences have been both challenging and rewarding. Whether I'm explaining the Holy Trinity to a class of inquisitive fourth graders or encouraging high schoolers to attend weekly Mass, I am blessed to have the opportunity to reflect on and explain the role of Christ in our lives.

I love when kids ask questions about our faith because it shows that they are interested and willing to grow in their Catholic faith. While I know that learning and living the faith should really be centered at home with family, I am glad that I am in a position to affirm our beliefs and be a positive influence on my students. I hope to lead by example and be a positive role model through whom the kids can see Christ at work.

—Owen

For Reflection

✳ Leading by example is what makes a person an authentic witness. Recall people who have been authentic witnesses for you. What made that person so real for you? How is God inviting you to be that kind of witness for others?

✳ Saint Paul wrote to the people in Corinth, "Be imitators of me, as I am of Christ" (1 Cor 11:1) to encourage them to be role models for one another. What does it take to be "a positive role model"? What are some characteristics of such a role model? Are you a positive role model to the people you encounter, or do some of your words and actions make it harder for others to see Christ? How can you become a better role model?

A LOVE THAT TRANSFORMS

Although I have been blessed to participate in mission opportunities throughout the world, the most transforming mission experience has been in my own city, Denver, Colorado. Many times people think that service work only happens in third world countries, like places in Africa or Central America. The result is that people can overlook the physically and emotionally hurting in their own backyards. No matter where we are, Christ asks us to serve one another in love; if we can do that, then God can and will do something beautiful.

Every year since I was in the eighth grade I have spent Holy Week working and sleeping at inner city parishes with my friends as part of Mission Youth Missions. During the three days leading up to Easter, we go door to door inviting people back to the Church, put on kids' camps at the parishes, assist at liturgies, paint, clean, and do whatever else the parish needs. By participating I was able to both be with my friends and experience Christ in mission.

This was what my experience had been until the year I met Ricky and Alex. I first saw Ricky and Alex while my friend and I dodged their paintball fire during one of the kids' camps. It wasn't the fact that they were shooting paintballs at us that surprised me. What shocked me was the steady stream of crude and disrespectful remarks they were hurling. I figured once they realized that we would be doing a lot of activities about our faith they wouldn't return. But they surprised me even more when they did. In fact, they were the first to arrive and the last to leave.

Ricky and Alex, along with their little gang of friends, were aggressive and mean to the other kids. They would speak out and fight with me and the other teen missionaries, and generally wreak havoc on what we were trying to do. During the first two days my patience was pushed to the very edge. I couldn't understand why the two of them kept coming back. By the grace of God, my friends and I didn't give up.

Every time I became frustrated with Ricky and Alex, I remembered that Jesus wanted me to love them. The real test of love comes when we are faced with those who are the most difficult to love. And for me, during that Holy Week, that was Ricky and Alex. So I did my best to love them, to show them acceptance, to model respecting people, and to explain who Christ is and why he died for us.

Whether we were playing football or just walking past one another, I saw Christ opening up moments for me to love them. Soon enough, I really did love those boys, and love helped them change.

Before long they began asking questions about God and their behavior became more respectful. Then, I began to understand *why* they kept coming back. Ricky and Alex had an unstable home life. I wondered if they had ever experienced love, or if anyone had ever challenged them, or taken interest in them, or just believed in them.

During the Easter Vigil, Ricky and Alex came with us to Mass. They were full of questions and they were soaking in the beauty of the Mass. In particular they were mesmerized by the Eucharist and their newfound knowledge that Jesus is truly present in the consecrated Bread and Wine.

When it came time for Communion, Ricky looked up at me and said, "Can I have him? Can I please eat the bread? I want Jesus in my heart." Since neither had yet received their first Communion, I told Ricky and Alex how the priest would give them a special blessing if they wanted, and Jesus would still be in their hearts. After Father blessed them, they walked back to their pews with a truly joyful look on their faces.

After Mass that night we took them to meet Father. He told them if they were willing to work hard this year, they could receive their first Communion next Easter. They swore that they would. "Anything, Father!" Ricky said enthusiastically. My friend and I walked home with them late that night. When we reached Ricky's house I looked at him and, bending down so we were face to face, made him pinky promise he would go to Church every Sunday and that he would never forget how much Jesus loves him. As Ricky promised, I watched his eyes fill with tears. He hugged me tightly as he looked up at me and said, "I love you."

I don't know where Ricky and Alex are now. But I hope—I have to believe—that they experienced

Christ in a way that changed them. Even if Ricky didn't keep his pinky promise, even if he never received his first Communion, that love—small as it might be in proportion to his pain—will last forever. Christ led me there, to those boys, for a reason. And they touched my heart more than they will ever know.

—*Mary Sarah*

For Reflection

✳ Jesus tells us to "love one another as I have loved you" (Jn 15:12). But loving other people is not always easy. Think of someone you find difficult to love. What are some things you can do to show love to this person as the son or daughter of God that they are? Pray for them and ask God to bless them and to give you the grace to see something "lovable" in them.

✳ Christ's love transformed Ricky and Alex. Jesus also wants to transform us. Read the story of Jesus and Zacchaeus (Lk 19:1–10) and imagine yourself in Zacchaeus's place. How does Jesus want to transform you with his love?

SERVANT LEADER

As a member of my school's campus ministry, I am one of the leaders helping to run a three-day retreat. Every summer incoming freshmen are required to attend this retreat to prepare them to become members of our Catholic school family. For the most part, they're either very nervous about it or completely against the idea of spending their last days of summer at a retreat.

During the retreat I saw how some of the freshmen acted during adoration. They were participating and opening their hearts to God. And as wonderful as that was to witness, what struck me the most is what I learned about being a "servant leader." As a student leader I, and the rest of the team, needed to put the needs of the teens on retreat before our own needs. We might be a bit older than they are, but we're still kids. To put them first wasn't easy, but seeing how God was making them a part of our faith family was well worth it.

—*Veronica M.*

For Reflection

✳ Those who answer the invitation to be at the service of others must still take time for their own needs—the need for quiet, prayer, rest, etc. How well do you balance your needs and the needs of others? How can you make sure to take the time you need so as to be able to better serve others? How can you encourage others to do the same?

✳ Sometimes the challenge of serving another is not the type of work we are doing, but that we feel we are not reaching the recipient. Recall a time when you felt someone was closed off. Put yourself in his or her shoes. Why might they have felt that way? What are some ways you can help create a sense of openness and welcome?

BEING A LIGHT

Seeing poverty up close for the first time hit me like a bus. I had spent a good amount of time in church, but had never really had the chance to experience poor people firsthand and help them. As a teenager from the suburbs, I had never seen bars on windows of houses or supermarkets until I went on mission trips to a very poor city in New Jersey for two summers.

There we were immersed in a world of poverty, a world I had never experienced before. There were syringes everywhere, gangs and prostitutes; I even heard gunshots nearby.

The signs of poverty and fear of danger taught me that sometimes service can be uncomfortable. It was sometimes a struggle to be kind to everyone. But the thing that makes it such a memorable place is the faith of the people who live there. As I worked, I just remembered the people's smiling faces and I could continue with a smile in my heart.

An experience that particularly struck me was when an elderly man, named Ivan, said, "God bless you." The fact that he would bless me, after knowing me for such a short time, left me speechless.

The Bible says, "Your light must shine before others, that they may see your good deeds and glorify your heavenly Father" (Mt 5:16). Being a missionary I was able to glorify God, help others, and help better myself. Because I went to New Jersey, I am a better Catholic, and, more importantly, a better person.

—*Liam*

For Reflection

✳ What does it mean to "glorify God?"

✳ Read Matthew 25:31–40. Ask Jesus: "How can I feed, welcome, and serve you in my daily life?" Thank Jesus for the chance to serve him every day through other people.

MESSAGE OF HOPE

When I was at the end of my sophomore year at a Catholic high school, I had the opportunity to go on a mission trip to a tribal reservation. I knew they wanted the group of us who were going to help run a week of Bible camp for children, but I didn't think much about what the trip entailed. I just knew that it would be a chance for me to do something different, so I decided to go. It didn't take long after arriving for me to realize that going was one of the best decisions I had ever made.

The bible camp took place at the Seven Dolors Church. We sang songs, did art projects, and spent a lot of time getting to know the kids. These children were different from the kids at the parishes in my hometown. Many of them didn't go to church regularly, they didn't have a "normal" family life, and they had already known more heartbreak than most people know in their lifetime. Witnessing the poverty and other difficult conditions that they experienced on a daily basis changed my life. What I experienced made reaching out to these kids so important that I have continued to volunteer at the reservation for a week each summer.

The children were so receptive to our message and to what we taught them about the faith; it was incredibly rewarding. But what has struck me the most was all they taught me. The children at this reservation carried with them a message of great hope. Though their lives were anything but easy, they continued to smile and view life as a gift. They also taught me to love with abandon. Too often I forget that it is in loving one another that I live for God, and not myself. And if God can continue to love me despite all of my flaws, who am I to deny love to those around me? I will forever remember with gratitude the children who showed me the importance of living with hope and loving with all my heart.

—*Christy*

For Reflection

✳ What does love with abandon mean to you? What would that look like in your daily life? In your relationships with family members, friends, and your community?

✳ Saying "yes" to God's call once led to the author saying "yes" again and again to her particular mission. Where in your life might God be calling you to continue with a particular mission? Pray for the resolve to say "yes" again and again.

A SIMPLE BROCHURE

It all started with a brochure a friend gave me. The brochure was for Haiti Christian Missions (HCM). It was a simple brochure asking for donations or service. I stashed it in my room and, although I saw it every day, I never really gave it a second thought.

Then several weeks later I heard about the earthquake that devastated Haiti. I was immediately struck with sadness thinking of the three million Haitians affected and offered many prayers for the victims. About a month later the desire to do something more for the people of Haiti continued to nag at me. I saw the brochure sitting where I had left it and called the number.

I started off saying, "I found a pamphlet at the back of my church. It gave me this number." From there the rest of the conversation was easy. I learned they needed volunteers and that they would be happy to meet with me and show me the ropes. I thanked God for getting me through this call and showing me a path I would never have considered. I called up my friend Rose and together we went to meet with HCM.

In addition to the questions about our age, we were asked if we could crochet, knit, or sew. They seemed pleased to hear that we could actually do all three. Then they explained how we could help. One woman, Mary, unpacked a box containing colorful plastic mats along with plastic shopping bags and many pairs of scissors.

"These," said Mary, "are bed mats. We made them for the homeless in Haiti before the earthquake, and now they need them even more." Mary went on to describe how the mats were made by cutting up shopping bags, tying them together, rolling them into "balls of yarn" and then crocheting them into mats.

At first it seemed complicated, but we quickly got the hang of it. Mary then pulled out a crocheted baby blanket and explained they also needed baby blankets for the nurseries in Haiti. Having made baby blankets before, Rose and I felt we could handle this project as well. Mary then pulled out the third and final project. It was a plastic bag filled with travel toiletries (i.e., travel-size toothpaste, toothbrush, shampoo, soap, and wash cloths). She explained that these personal care kits were put together for those in the hospitals who didn't have the money to care for themselves.

After thanking them for their time and promising to keep in touch, Rose and I left with two huge garbage bags stuffed with shopping bags, huge crochet hooks, and another garbage bag filled with yarn. Before going home, we made a quick stop at the dollar store. After purchasing enough toiletries for twenty kits, we went home eager to get started. Rose and I were busy almost every free minute we had crocheting, knitting, and making personal care kits. Our friends were very supportive too! Many of them took the time to join us in making blankets, collecting bags, and crocheting mats as well.

After five months we had made ten plastic bed mats, twenty baby blankets, and hundreds of personal care kits. We were getting low on plastic bags and really wanted to keep helping HCM. Since many people simply throw out plastic shopping bags, Rose and I sent out a standard letter to everyone living in our area asking them to drop off their spare plastic bags at our addresses. We also included my email address just in case someone wanted to get in touch with us. A day later we had around seventy-five bags. A week later we had collected more than we could store. We brought our finished mats, blankets, personal care kits, and a trunk load of bags to HCM. They were so happy!

Several days later, a women's auxiliary club emailed me and said they wanted me to come and speak at one of their meetings. I was shocked and overjoyed that they would ask me to speak about what Rose and I were doing. Armed with a computer presentation and sample mats, kits, and blankets, I spoke to the ladies about HCM. The presentation went very well and, by the end, every lady offered to cut plastic bags for us. They also presented us with a basket filled with toiletries they had purchased! I was shocked, not only was I spreading the word about the great work HCM was doing, but everybody was being so generous with donations. I knew God always provides, and their actions confirmed how God was working through us.

We continued making the mats, blankets, and care packages. A few months after I spoke to the women's auxiliary club, Rose got a phone call asking if she and I could come and speak to a class of third graders. We packed up all our materials again and headed out to the school, eager to see the reactions of younger children. We started talking and, by the end of our presentation, every third grader had their mouths open and were hungry to hear more. When we started teaching them how to cut the plastic bags they were even more interested. We stayed for the morning and when we were leaving, the teacher asked if we could leave some bags for her class to continue to cut. We agreed with enthusiasm, grateful to have other people doing the cutting (it did get tiring after a while). We knew the children listened to us but had no clue how seriously they wanted to take on this new mission.

After the presentation one boy went home and told his mother about us. Later that week Rose got an email from the mother asking if we would be able to speak at her church. We said yes and found ourselves speaking to another crowd of ladies who also cut bags for us. Another surprise was what the mother of the boy brought—ten balls of plastic that were cut and rolled by her son's class! Rose and I were astonished by their generosity—we didn't even expect one ball.

We continued to volunteer for HCM, meeting with Mary and her crew once a month to give them what was finished. In late December, I found out my family was moving far away from any HCM location. I really wanted to start up one in my new location but, after looking into the matter, I realized it would be much too expensive to start by myself. I felt sad but I decided to do one last major project as a "goodbye." I sent out a letter again, dropping them in neighbor's mailboxes. This time instead of asking for bags, I asked for personal care package fillers.

I knew people may not respond to this request as much, because they actually had to buy things. I was surprised at the results and was able to make fifty personal care packages with the donations from my neighbors. Volunteering with HCM has strengthened my faith and taught me it is possible to love people I have never met. And it all started with a simple, little, forgotten brochure—God took my desire to help and nurtured it into something beautiful!

—Cassie

For Reflection

❋ In Matthew's Gospel, Jesus takes five loaves of bread and two fish and multiplies them to feed more than 5,000 people. How did God take Cassie's small desire to help others and multiply it into something bigger?

❋ The brochure in this story was just one small nudge from God, and yet it became a community-wide project. What are possible nudges from God in your life? What do you imagine he might think you (and your community) are capable of? Take one small sign you might have overlooked and list three ways you can grow this particular mission.

SPEAKING THE RIGHT LANGUAGE

I was standing on a dreary plot of land that was a playground of an inner city school where I volunteer. More than thirty kindergartners were running carelessly, vying for a turn to go down the slide within the intimidating chain-link-fence enclosure. I waited for one of them to trip and skin a knee or for one to come and tattle on another when I was caught off guard.

I felt a small set of hands tugging on the back of my shirt. I turned around and was immediately grasped in a firm hug by a little girl. Her name was Carmen and she was having a rough day. When I asked her what was wrong she told me, "I hate school." In the short conversation that followed, I quickly realized that attempting to communicate with her in English was not going to work, so I switched to Spanish.

What came next, in response to my prodding, was an explanation of Carmen's anxiety about not speaking English well. She said that her teachers taught in English so even if she could follow the lesson (which was an uncommon occurrence), she was unable to participate or ask questions due to her fear and embarrassment over her choppy English. Carmen needed a teacher who spoke her language— we all do. We all need to have teachers who we understand and who understand what we need to learn.

Hearing Carmen's predicament made me think of how Jesus speaks my language. Jesus understands me and knows what I need to learn even if I'm not aware of it. I often arrive at this after-school program thinking that I am there to minister to the children. In a sense it's true: I help to supervise them, make sure they get dinner, help them do homework, and hopefully I serve as a positive role model for them. But in another sense they minister to me; they show me the face of Jesus in a way that words cannot capture.

Something about these children speaks to my heart about Jesus's love for each one of us. Through them Jesus teaches me that his love is never earned and never diminishes. Through them I have learned that they and all of us are God's beloved children, created in his image and dwelling places of the Holy Spirit. Seeing them as God's precious daughters and sons (rather than burdensome, undocumented residents as they are often identified), moves me to action knowing that in serving them, I am serving Christ, and that through them Christ is serving and teaching me.

—Frankie

For Reflection

✳ Read Psalm 139:1–14. Take a moment to ponder the beauty of your creation in all its complexities— your mind, your body, your heart. Praise God for the good things, the gifts that he has given you. How can knowing we are all wonderfully made and formed in God help us in our call to mission?

✳ Call to mind the image of someone you have helped. Do you see Christ in them? Do you think they saw Christ in you? If the answer is "no," pray, asking God to give you a new way of seeing, one that reveals him in each and every one of us.

GUIDED BY THE SPIRIT

Have you ever felt a deep and desperate yearning in your heart to help other people? Maybe you wanted to assist a friend in a bad relationship; maybe you want to help your family whom you see every day; or maybe approach the kid in school whose mom just died. Maybe you see your friend dying on the inside, and you just wish you could tell her that happiness isn't wrapped up in the boy who cheated on her last Saturday.

I have had this feeling many times, and it made me angry that I couldn't seem to make a difference in the world. I've played ideas of ways to help friends, family, and others over and over in my mind. After reading a blog and becoming kind of obsessed with the blogger's creativity, I was inspired to start my own blog.

On May 17, I wrote my first blog post about a profound experience of charity. I started the blog for the purpose of telling the world that there is a light in the darkness. I wanted to share Christ with my generation. I began blogging when I was fifteen years old, and have been blogging for over a year now. I hope my blog portrays what it means to be a vibrant, young, Catholic teen. Everything in my blog hopefully serves to tell others about how to be faith-filled witnesses in our world. I feel that the Holy Spirit guides my blog because there is no way I could have expressed by myself how my faith is such an integral part of my life.

—Faith

For Reflection

✳ Think about times you have wanted to help someone. What did you do? How do you think you can continue to serve in this way for longer periods?

✳ Pentecost was a moment of "great commission." With the help of the Holy Spirit, the apostles were able to evangelize in many different languages so a great number could be saved. This author communicates God's message through her blog. How do you communicate the Holy Spirit's work in your life? What does he want you to say? How will you respond to the "great commission"?

GIFT OF LOVE

When I think about the summer right after my freshman year of college, I don't think of relaxing by the pool. I don't think of beach days, or summer love. I don't think of barbecues. I remember the day I woke up in India—hot, sweating, jet-lagged, and surrounded by a mosquito net—to the sound of the Muslim call to prayer. It was 4:30 AM. We would leave in an hour for our first day of working with the Missionaries of Charity.

I have always felt a special connection to Blessed Mother Teresa. We share a birthday, and I grew up to be just as short as she was. When the woman who ran my Bible study told me that she was leading a trip to Kolkata, India, to continue Mother Teresa's work, I knew I was supposed to be on that trip. Eight months and about twenty hours of flying later, it was my first day.

I decided to work at *Prem Dan*, meaning "Gift of Love," a home for the sick, dying, and disabled.

Immediately, I was thrown into a whirlwind of
confusion and disarray, hard physical labor and even
harder emotional burdens. I felt lost. I felt so useless.
I had come to India to make a difference and to help.
What help could I be with a hundred women yelling
for a multitude of things in a language I didn't
understand? I mulled that thought over every day at
Mother Teresa's tomb, during Mass at the Mother
House, and during our daily holy hour.

As time passed, though, I saw my purpose in
the form of a special friendship formed with one of
the patients, Niruala. Bright and vibrant in a place
where there was a lot of despair, we connected by
making faces at each other and mimicking actions.
If she danced, I danced. If I stuck my tongue out,
so did she. The love she had helped to release my
own. No longer was a task just physical labor, but
one of pouring out as much love as possible through
my hands. I started to realize that love has so
many forms. Sometimes love was feeding patients.
Other times, it was helping them use the toilet.
When I released myself from holding back my own
love, I saw my relationships with Niruala, fellow

missionaries, God, and myself grow. I was no longer afraid of letting love out.

I went to India hoping to change things, to make a difference. And isn't that the reason most of us go on mission trips—to fix things for people who have no ability to repay us? But, what I realized is that India helped to fix me. Yes, I did a lot for other people. I went up and kissed a leper everyone else tried to avoid. I lived the corporal works of mercy in feeding the hungry and caring for the sick. But, in loving with everything I had, I released in myself a power I didn't know was there and began to heal my own heart. And isn't that what the Prayer of St. Francis of Assisi means when it says, "for it is in giving that we receive?"

On my last day at *Prem Dan*, I was beside myself with emotions. Niruala was ill and I would never know how it turned out for her. At the very end of the day, I grabbed a Missionary of Charity and asked her to please translate my goodbyes to the one who started my own healing. I told Niruala that I was leaving, and that I didn't think I'd ever be back. Immediately, as sick as she was, she propped herself up, held my face, and kissed me. Nothing ever before or since had a greater impact on me. For so many weeks, I had felt that I was only a drop in the ocean. That even with everything I did, it didn't change anything. But it did for one little woman who liked to dance.

On my trip to Kolkata I saw Jesus in the faces of the people society forgot to love. But, the really transformative thing was my own ability to recognize Jesus in myself. In a life full of self-consciousness and perfectionism, that has been very hard for me. I never thought I would mean that much to Niruala or the other workers at *Prem Dan*. To pour out my own love and receive theirs truly opened my heart to receive God's love.

God works through each and every one of us. I hope one day we can all see our own beauty and worth in the eyes of our Heavenly Father, and the worth of his other children who surround us.

—*Marie I.*

For Reflection

✳ Have you seen the face of Jesus in others? If so, when and how? Have you ever been able to see Christ in yourself?

✳ Even though we may feel like just one tiny part of an immense whole, God values our existence and how we complete it. Spend some time allowing yourself to feel his love working in you and through you.

PRAYER BEFORE MISSION

Lord, you sent your disciples out into the world over 2000 years ago, and now you send me. As I reach out to others in your name, I ask you to accompany me every step of the way. Love them through me, and show me how to treat them with the respect and dignity they deserve. Help me to see you in the faces of my brothers and sisters. And let them see your face in mine. Amen.

PRAYER AFTER MISSION

I am tired after a long day, Lord. And yet, before I give in completely to exhaustion, I want to thank you. For the blessing of serving others in your name, I praise you. For the ability to recognize that the world is bigger than just me, I thank you. And for the courage to love my brothers and sisters in big and little ways, I am grateful. I ask that you continue to bless the people I served today, and that you make use of both my gifts and limitations. Amen.

CHECKLIST FOR MISSION

Things to Bring

- ☐ who you really are
- ☐ an open mind and heart
- ☐ joy and enthusiasm
- ☐ good sense of humor
- ☐ a willingness to work
- ☐ your relationship with God
- ☐ team spirit
- ☐ a desire to both give and receive
- ☐ commitment to cooperation

- ☐ things that help you pray

Things to Leave Behind

- [ ] negativity
- [ ] laziness
- [ ] preconceived notions
- [ ] expectations
- [ ] desire for attention
- [ ] pride

     (e.g., thinking that anything is beneath you)

- [ ] prejudices and any sense of superiority

- [ ] your comfort zone

Acknowledgments

This book only exists because of the many incredible teens who submitted reflections on their experiences of mission. We are humbled to have received and read so many inspiring witnesses to God's call for young people today. Unfortunately, we were not able to use all of the submissions sent to us; but, we extend our heartfelt gratitude to each person who contributed.

We are especially thankful for the teachers, youth group leaders, and others involved in teen ministry who are serving the amazing teens in their lives and who helped us by collecting these reflections: Wayne Burbach (St. Elizabeth Ann Seton Parish, Maryland), Amy Chapman (St. Ignatius Parish, Massachusetts), Jaclyn Torres (Junipero Serra High School, California), Jeff Finnegan (Bl. Teresa of Calcutta Parish, Missouri), Bill Gavin (Holy Trinity Parish, Virginia), Ignitum Today (ignitumtoday.com), Jeff Kacala (St. Katharine Drexel Parish, Wisconsin), Mike Kilgannon (Holy Name Parish, Massachusetts), John Paul Manning (St. Mary of the Assumption

Parish, Massachusetts), Chris McCormick (St. Teresa Parish, Florida), The Office of St. Louis Youth Ministry, *Radiant* magazine (be-radiant.com), Sandy Reynolds (Kennedy Catholic, Missouri), Rob Ryan (Ascension Parish, Missouri), Emily Shull (All Saints Parish, Missouri), Julia Strukely (Bishop Ireton High School, Virginia), Kate Sweeney (Regis Jesuit High School, Illinois), Jennessa Terracino (former youth minister, Virginia), Chris Turner (Life Teen, lifeteen. com), Julie Anne Walker and Margie Weir (Holy Name of Jesus Parish, Florida), Lindsey Webb (St. Catherine of Siena Parish, Massachusetts), Father Tom Yehl (Seton School, Virginia).

For assisting with the writing of reflection questions, we would also like to express our appreciation for the young women of the Pauline Discipleship program: Karen Barnett, Michelle Chandy, Joanna Corea, Amanda Detry, Melissa Fisackerly, Janet Gonzalez, and Paulina Pesqueira.

And, of course, our sincerest thanks to all the teens who shared their reflections.

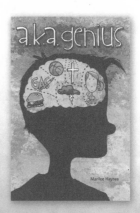